Lukasz Luczaj

ON THE WILD SIDE

From the Anthropology of
Hunter-Gatherers to Postmodern
Foraging, Bushcraft and New-Age
Nature Seekers

Pietrusza Wola 2020

ISBN 9781713423997

Self-published on Kindle Direct Publishing

English translation of the revised edition of
Łuczaj Ł. (2010) *W dziką stronę*,
Krośnieńska Oficyna Wydawnicza, Krosno,
translated by Nasim Łuczaj.

Cite this book as: Luczaj, L. 2020. *On the Wild Side: From the Anthropology of Hunter-Gatherers to Postmodern Foraging, Bushcraft and New-Age Nature Seekers.*

Contact with the author:
www.thewildfood.org, www.luczaj.com

Table of Contents

A long, long time ago, it must be twenty years now, I went to the park in Dukla. Not without reason: in spring, the whole park reeks of the wild cousin of what we call garlic, known as ramsons, wild garlic or bear's garlic. Local people used to call different wild herbs bear's, hare's, or sparrow's, and garlic happened to be given the epithet 'bear's'. It doesn't need planting or collecting, it grows in large fields, and you can simply come and pick a few juicy leaves, shaped like leaves of the lily of the valley with the taste of the best chives. I was picking this wild garlic like some Russian or Georgian would (two nations which have a liking for this vegetable) when an old lady walked up to me. She waved her walking stick at me and said, 'Sir, don't eat that, it's wild, it may harm you!'.

The more human civilization develops, the more often the theme of return to nature, to the natural and the wild, appears in art and media as a lost good. The conviction that the present is 'worse' than the past is as old as humankind itself. The Ancient Greeks also believed in a 'golden age of mankind'. They were followed by many more thinkers, with Jean-Jacques Rousseau at their forefront, who studied the subject of wildness and sensed a dissonance between what is natural and what is 'artificial'. I myself spent many years trying to understand the term. In the meantime, the last hunter-gatherer tribes on Earth were undergoing gradual extermination.

This book is meant to be an assemblage of notes and thoughts seized in haste: just after a walk, on the train, in the plane, in the forest, sitting on a hilltop, after breakfast. It forms a thematic whole but can be read in any order, much like a poetry collection or an encyclopaedia. My first attempt at a work about the 'wild human' was a text I wrote several years ago for the online esoteric magazine Taraka, entitled 'A seasonal return to a Paleolithic way of life as a new form of sacred time'.

More recent studies in the disciplines of medicine and psychology show how beneficial the maximalisation of habits that resemble primitive ways of life can be for human wellbeing. These include a diet rich in protein, based on good quality lean meat and wild plants rich in nutrients, a diet low in sugar and fat, an active lifestyle, breastfeeding children for a long time, and belonging to a small group with strong emotional ties. Maybe soon the great importance of periodic fasting, cruel initiation rites and shamanic trance will also be 'scientifically' proven and will be as obvious as holidays by the sea.

The terms 'natural' and 'wild' have many, often conflicting, meanings. Reflection on these, though unlikely to lead to a breakthrough on a worldwide scale, may well improve individuals' quality of life and help them to develop a sense of happiness.

I wrote a book about the wild and the natural because the subject has baffled me for my whole life. Trying to be wilder and more natural, acting on internal instincts, I gradually came to realise how difficult, complicated, and multiple in meanings these tasks are. Although there are many things I haven't managed to accomplish, my search for nature has widened my horizons in life and filled it with primitive joy.

There are many references to the natural world in this book. For good reason: I was educated as a biologist – I am an ecologist and ethnobotanist. However, I am writing not just from a scientific perspective, but from the point of view of someone who has really searched for wildness, who lives in the countryside, who seeks to return to ancient techniques and spends a lot of their time on the grass, looking at the sky.

Into the wild

While I was beginning to consider writing something on the subject, Jon Krakauer's book *Into the Wild* and the film based on it became immensely popular. The book is a deeply lyrical analysis of the life story of a certain Christopher McCandless. This man, young and prone to solitary travel, decided to completely cut himself off from civilization for some time and set off deep into Alaska with a rucksack, sleeping bag, gun, and a few other accessories. His body was later found in his sleeping bag in a bus wreck in the middle of a vast Alaskan forest.

This poor young man became a symbol for those who search for nature and wildness. Many people wrote or said to me: 'You know that book *Into the Wild*? He's a bit like you!'. But what does 'a bit' mean? For some time I dreamed of doing something similar, of isolating myself somewhere in the Carpathian mountains, but at that point I already had a wife and my first daughter, a safety net, something to connect me with humanity. I am also fascinated with finding food in the wild, and when I was around McCandless' age I had a beard of similar length and a similarly crazy look in the eye. I never got to the extreme experience of spending a winter alone in the taiga, forced to hunt for animals. I did things gradually, so it was also gradually that I came to understand my weaknesses. These resulted both from the necessity of many years of preparation, the natural weakness of any single human being destined to years of struggle with the elements, and from my own physical limitations – I was always the worst in class at PE, I could only run faster than two overweight kids and could never catch the ball. The only thing I could do as well as other boys was to throw the ball into the net. I never really understood my predicament. I even had some tests done, expecting I might have a heart condition. But everything was all right. Maybe it's a deficiency on the level of cellular respiration? Some mitochondrial dysfunction that made me awkward weird, strong in my weakness and sensitive to spirits and ghosts?

Many people, usually young men, have tried and continue to try to escape civilization at some point in their lives. Many returned after a single night in the woods, others after a month, some after a year or two of wandering. McCandless gained fame because of his death, which was mainly the result of a lack of preparation and knowledge of his surroundings. Wild tribes live in places that they have, as a rule, known since childhood. Whether hot or cold, they live in the climate they grew up in. The spirits of their ancestors, who died in these territories, are also their allies. Raging young Westerners usually (though not always) escape to places to which they have never been before.

Chris McCandless was running away from both people and the system. Yet he took with him one of its criminal elements – a firearm, as well as a modern sleeping bag and a camera, which he used to document his final days.

Krakauer devotes at least a chapter of his book to considerations about the reasons behind McCandless' death. The film leans towards the interpretation that he ate poisonous plants. But the truth is more complicated and, as Krakauer writes, there were most likely a few factors at play: his injury, the cold, and perhaps an accumulation of poison from the plants he ate. As someone who has been eating plants for many years now, I know that with the exception of very poisonous plants, our body only signals their harmfulness gradually. Plants which don't make us feel good after eating them slowly become sort of less tasty. But McCandless was stubborn and had little choice. It's also worth remembering about so-called rabbit starvation, that is, death from eating nearly exclusively lean meat, which is made up of almost exclusively protein. After a few days of such a diet, the body reacts with vomiting and weakness.

It might be hard for someone inexperienced at sourcing food to survive, even if armed. Wild animals do not contain much fat, and protein itself contains less calories than fat does. Game is much less rich in calories than the fat meat of bred pigs or cows. Living in 'natural' conditions, being in constant movement and subject to cold temperatures, we would need around 2 kg of game per day to survive. It is easy to calculate just how many animals we would have to kill, unless we have bison, elk, or elephants at our disposal. Besides, killing such a large animal is no guarantee of success either, for it takes a lot of work to preserve such a large amount of meat, for example by drying or smoking it. Chris McCandless experienced this when he hunted an elk. A lot of the meat went to waste, eaten by maggots.

Raymond Maufrais experienced similar difficulties when hunting, in his case mainly for small forest birds. His books *Aventures en Guyane* and *Aventures au Mato grosso* are shocking accounts of his two solitary journeys through the jungles of South America. He did not survive the second journey. He left only a journal behind. The journal's subject was incredibly worn out by frequent tropical rainfall and other inconveniences of his surroundings. In addition, he suffered from malnutrition, most likely so-called rabbit starvation, caused by the consumption of solely lean meat.

We should ask ourselves to what extent an escape deep into the forest with factory-made weapons, a camera, a sleeping bag, and a pair of Wellington boots is indeed an escape from civilization. The McPhersons are in a good position to understand this. They are a married couple and authors of a book with a similar title: *Naked into the Wilderness*. This is not, however, a diary from their journey towards death, or a record of two years of survival in the forest, but a guide on how to survive and do everything without owning anything at all. The authors are so orthodox that even when they are explaining how to light a fire with a bow drill, they provide instructions for how to make the bowstring out of your own (long!) hair, or from plant fibres. Of course if you are going to use a knife, it can only be made out of stone or a horn...

Alaska itself, famed for its wildness, is a place to which many adventurers have tried to make a solitary escape from civilization. For example, Krakauer mentions the case of a daredevil who built a hut deep in the Alaskan wilderness and managed to stock up on food for the winter but incorrectly calculated how much food he would need and starved to death by February, apparently without trying too hard to save his life (there was a hut stocked up on food three miles downstream).

Krakauer gives another example: that of Gene Rosellini, an incredibly talented man from a rich family who went to university, where he received very good grades, and attended courses in anthropology, history, philosophy, and linguistics. However, he didn't finish his studies because he never saw the need to, even though he passed most of his subjects. He abandoned his degree and set off on a journey along the West Coast, towards Alaska. In 1977, he settled in a forest near the town of Cordova. Ten years later, he explained in an interview that he was living like his primitive ancestors. He did away with nearly all of the advances of his civilization with the conviction that as the human race advances, it is in fact slowly degrading. He experimented with different stages of human development until he finally reached the Neolithic stage. I suppose this means he cultivated some plants (otherwise he would have boasted about being Paleolithic).

Rosellini maintained this way of life for over a decade. Towards the end of this period, as it seems to follow from a surviving letter to his friend, he gave up on the idea of full success and decided to set off on a permanent voyage around the world, on foot. In the end, he never left 'his' forest. He committed suicide in 1991.

A seasonal return to a Paleolithic lifestyle as the new form of sacred time

In the beginning, humans were hunter-gatherers. In small groups, they led a nomadic or semi-nomadic existence. People lived in simple, often temporary shelters, gathered few goods and made little provisions, and ate whatever they could find and catch. Primitive human culture was nomadic, egalitarian, and only based on ownership to a small extent. What was 'owned' were social relationships, ways of adjusting to the ecosystem, and relationships with the spiritual world. Does this idea make sense? Humans' primitive spirituality was animistic and shamanic. One didn't have to 'believe' in the spiritual world – it was just there. The belief in the animated and soul-possessing nature of objects was widespread. Getting in touch with such a nature and altered states of mind was easier thanks to the following factors: the animistic worldview itself, periodic shortages of food ('fasting from necessity'), often uncomfortable shelters which disturbed the sleeping period in a way that would blur the distinction between waking life and sleep (the opposite of an alarm clock), a diet based on meat and low-calorie plants which prevented the rationalising effect of high blood sugar, as well as a high level of knowledge about psychoactive plants and mushrooms. Furthermore, the hunter's ethos encouraged cruel initiations and other physical challenges that placed the human being on the verge of death. The very meagreness of tools and resources encouraged a direct 'relationship with reality', both in terms of the physical (blood) and the ghost world.

Changes that took place in most societies over the past few thousand years, which are characterised by the domestication of plants and animals, permanent human settlements, and eventually an increase in the comfort of life and sleep, material goods and size of communities, had a large, greatly rationalising influence on human behaviour.

While in small, traditional hunter-gatherer and primitive farming communities the festive season – sacred time as opposed to profane time – is, with the exception of initiation rituals, a time when people come together in larger groups, a time of rest after hunting or gathering, sometimes even after preparation for these, the situation is very different in wealthy post-industrial societies. Here holidays or longer amounts of free time, as opposed to, for instance, Christmas, a relic of traditional festivities, become a time for a kind of 'intensification of experience'.

The monotony of everyday working life and the activities it involves are replaced with becoming someone else. Christmas Eve in Poland used to, to a large extent, revolve around food. Malnourished societies treated food as sacred. Our fairly well-fed society increasingly shifts the emphasis from schematic and ritualised traditional festivities to those based on opportunities for self-expression, a return to a way of life that suits us best from an evolutionary point of view, or a chance to catch up on initiations.

I dare say that the most common way of spending such free time, a new expression used to signify holy days, is a return to a primitive way of life. Sometimes we are aware of this return, for example when we go on all kinds of survival or Native-Americanizing workshops or meetings, but usually it happens automatically, without us realizing. Here we should take note of the nomadisation of holidays and the desire to move around and travel, especially combined with camping. We go on all sorts of fishing trips or mushroom picking (direct forms of hunting and gathering) as well as participate in more veiled forms of primitive activities (safaris, looking at coral reefs, trips to the zoo, etc.). Strangely enough, the release from large social organisms (corporations, schools, offices) is accompanied by an intensification of interpersonal relationships – new acquaintances, friendships, romances. People go back to small social structures, consisting of a few or just over a dozen people (walking trips, coach trips, travelling with friends).

So far, anthropologists have identified two main hypothetical primitive habitats of the *Homo sapiens*. One of these is the savannah, the other are coasts of seas and lakes, which are rich in molluscs and fish. Of course, both the savannah and such waters exist in hot climates. Every year, Europe bears witness to an exodus towards these primitive human habitats. Rock music, hippie, techno festivals, as well as medieval knight tournaments, motorbike and racing rallies, or even sites for meetings with the Pope share a common trait – they all take place in large, savannah-like, amphitheatrical grassy spots, usually with the odd tree dotted around them. Those who don't attend any of the above spend their time in traffic jams on the motorway or in airport queues on their way to the hot beaches of southern Europe and other sunny shores. There, half-naked or naked, relishing their seafood, grilled fish, grapes or mango, dancing in nightclubs on ecstasy, they are maybe a little closer to their ancestors than when in front of the computer screen or at their school desk on an overcast, snowy January day.

The recently developed field of evolutionary medicine tries to prevent illnesses through teaching people how to live in accord with an evolutionarily worked-out primitive way of life in the modern world. This involves, among other things, a lot of movement and a diet rich in leaves, fruits, and lean meats.

But what has this got to do with spirituality? A lot. First of all, often the self-realization that we are more primitive and closer to our imagined roots than we thought, as well as our sense of return to a golden age, become goals in themselves and we treat our holidays as a sacred time. Furthermore, this sacred free time is a prerequisite for alterations in consciousness. Free time is a time when we turn off our alarms. Our natural sleep cycle isn't drastically interrupted, and that's when we tend to remember dreams. Saturday dreams are often the most meaningful dreams. It's a time for winding down, meditation, prayer, yoga, pilgrimage, but also a time for madness. You're able to spend 24 hours in front of a screen, go to nightclubs, or hitchhike around Europe. Free time is time for finding something new, for a renewal of spontaneous relationships with people, nature, and spirituality. It's a time when we subconsciously seek out liminal situations, borderlines, openness, risk, the unidentified. Hitchhiking, travel, drugs, or even leaving the socio-natural environments that surround us from day to day, are situations like this. Sometimes dangerous ones – the greatest number of car accidents occurs during the summer holidays.

Up to this point, this piece has revolved around situations in which we are not consciously aware of the sacred and liminal aspects of our holidays. But what about approaching this consciously? With a prepared mindset, a little theatrically. Wisely combining or separating the initational-deprivational and orgiastic-carnavalistic aspects of sacred time. I don't know whether this would improve our experiences or spoil the fun. What if we make walking trips to the savannah in Africa (for weight loss and transformation) – combined with fishing, orgies and techno parties, and preceded by a sadomasochistic initiation – something as sacred and traditional as Christmas Eve? That's something I'm happy to discuss.

What does 'natural' mean?

The adjective 'natural' is closely tied to the adjective 'primitive'. Natural means in accord with nature, primitive – the way something was originally, in the beginning. Assuming that humans are becoming less and less 'natural', we should seek the exemplar natural human in the primitive human.

This reminds me of a certain scientific conference (the 37th Geobotanical Conference), which took place in Warsaw in 1992 as part of a gathering of the Geobotanical Section of the Polish Botanical Society, entitled 'The primeval nature of Polish wildlife'. Its organiser, professor Janusz Faliński, considered it to be of enough importance to have a transcript of its recording published in the journal *Phytocoenosis* [1] . The speakers – plant ecologists and archaeologists – debated on the issue of identifying the point at which the natural world in Poland ceased to be primeval. Was it twelve thousand years ago, when the last glacier began to melt and the population started to increase? Only back then it was still tundra... Were the forests that formed later, first of a birch-pine taiga type, then coming to include oak, linden, or elm, still natural? Or was the influence of humans two or three thousand years ago small enough for the forest, at least in parts of the country, to count as primeval? Is the Białowieża National Park, the last remaining forest to be nearly untouched by human hand in the European Plain, natural?

I remember wondering where to do my Masters. Professor Andrzej Batko recommended the Białowieża Forest, where I would be under the supervision of professor Faliński, because aside from the incredible character of the latter, 'I would have a point of reference for the rest of my life', 'I will know what is meant by a natural forest', and 'no-one will be able to convince me that just any forest is natural', said Batko. I listened to him.

I went to the Forest. I was nineteen. I'd wandered around the Carpathians before and I'd seen many beautiful

---

[1] Falinski J.B. (ed.) 1993. PIERWOTNOŚĆ PRZYRODY Zapis Seminarium Geobotanicznym,Warszawa, 29 lutego 1992 r
Phytocoenosis 5 (N.S.) *Seminarium Geobotanicum* 2.

forests in my lifetime. But the Białowieża Forest surprised me, at first with its dead wood – there were half-rotten tree trunks all over the place. They were covered with ferns, moss, mushrooms, and even young trees. There were large pits of water made in spots where toppled spruces used to lie. Commercial forests thrive on euthanasia. When the time comes, all the trees die in the same way – cut down with a chainsaw. Here, trees had different deaths. Some species, such as pines, would dry up and stay standing for years, like ghosts. Others, such as linden and aspen, would break in half. Finally, the wind would uproot the spruce. There was less verticality in that forest, the trees didn't look like an army standing to attention. It was a battlefield, or maybe a drunken dance in some primitive rite. Vertical trees, dead horizontal trees, nearly horizontal trees with new vertical trunks growing out of them. Slanted trees. Trees growing on top of each other. Coniferous trees on metre-long, rotten trunks. Hollows made by windthrow which you could drown in. Dead linden, empty inside, in which you could spend the night.

If you counted the number of plant species in this forest, there would turn out to be a similar amount as in a 'near-natural' forest, any old reserve or well-kept commercial forest. But this kind of forest has a different geometry, as well as more saprophytic fungi on dead wood, grubs, and other larvae. These aspects of the natural forest are more present. Aurochs and wild boar, deer, wolves, foxes and lynx all live in this Forest. Bears died out many years ago. Is a wild forest, untouched by the axe, with wolves and aurochs but no bears, a natural forest? Apparently wolverines, which are now only able to live in the far North, also may have lived here. Maybe the

21

Białowieża Forest is only complete and natural if it includes wolverines? Animals can make a strong mark on vegetation. Each year, wild boars dig up a large portion of the Forest, which in some areas looks like an arable field with a few trees in it. They transport the rhizomes of forest flowers on their snouts. The seeds of some plants sprout from auroch dung. Beavers cut down entire riverside groves of trees.

Only a hundred years ago, most forest regions far away from smoky villages were covered in a coat of lichen of the *Usnea* genus. Currently *Usnea* can be found as a rarity in the north-east corner of Poland. They are very rare in the rest of the country. A relatively large amount of this sort of lichen can be found on the coasts of Western Europe, for instance in Scotland. The air that comes from the sea, most often brought by western winds, is very clean there. Most species of lichen are known to be incredibly sensitive to even the slightest air pollution.

The savannah, the sea, and children

The stereotype of the savannah as humanity's first motherland came to prominence in the last few decades. Close your eyes. A large grassy space with single trees and bushes, lions, elephants, and antelopes comes to mind...

Edward Tylor, one of the founding fathers of cultural anthropology, who studied the origins of religion and coined the term *animism*, was highly interested in children's natural inclinations. He believed that the origins of humanity are in some way preserved in the behaviour and dispositions of children. He mainly had in mind all sorts of childish and magical forms of thinking. Perhaps children's dispositions will also be able to reveal us the ecological motherland of humanity? Children, as well as adults, enjoy open spaces dotted with trees. The park landscape of the savannah is a landscape humans feel comfortable in. Children like to go to the park... There's often a sandpit in parks and city green spaces. Children love sand. They love sand by the sea, beaches, the ocean, and the vicinity of water in general.

The oceanographer Alister Hardy formulated a hypothesis about the relationship between human evolution and water back in 1930, but he first presented it 30 years later. His main argument was the presence of a thick layer of fat on humans, just like on many marine mammals. His opponents, however, defend the savannah theory by claiming that fat was also required on the savannah to keep naked bodies warm during cold nights. Elaine Morgan is another proponent of the aquatic ape theory. Her arguments include: traces of interdigital webbing between fingers, tear glands akin to marine animals, the ability to swim and to control breath. It should be noted that the savannah and the aquatic ape hypotheses can be combined somehow. Perhaps we first evolved by the water and then moved to the savannah. Or maybe we are creatures adjusted to two habitats?

Assuming that humans are omnivores, the coast should be their best habitat. Living in such a place, they can not only penetrate the land, including the forest or the savannah, but also obtain very precious food from marine animals, for instance fish, shellfish, mussels, as well as seaweed. Some tropical seashores also have mangroves – forests of trees with trunks raised by protruding roots which allow for the trees' growth in floodplains. These forests, which can be found for instance in Indochina, are a very rich source of food and a habitat for many species of marine animals.

The aquatic ape theory and its hypothesis about the relationship between the primitive human and water was, for many years, made fun of by the majority of archaeologists. Most discoveries of human ancestors come from far inland, especially the highlands of the west of Africa. However, it is of course possible that coastal human remains were destroyed as a result of rising sea levels. A very important argument in favour of the importance of the sea in the expansion of primitive humans comes from the Americas, which have only recently been settled, and Native Americans are not genetically diverse. How, then, did they manage to colonise such a large territory? Assuming that their ancestors reached Tierra del Fuego from Asia through Alaska and the Bering Strait, they would have had to colonise incredibly diverse environments: the taiga, deciduous forests, steppes, semi-deserts, tropical forests and rainforests. It turns out that there are traces which point to America's colonization having begun along the coastline. Beds of edible molluscs, for example the especially abundant and easy-to-collect mussels, can be found along the entire coast of the Americas, from Alaska to Tierra del Fuego. The first Native American families travelled a few dozen kilometres or further without having to change their ways of getting food. They were able to access ever-new resources of molluscs and fish. Ecotone environments – the verges of two ecosystems – are incredibly rich and appealing environments for humans. Canadian researchers Nancy Turner, Iain J. Davidson-Hunt, and Michael O'Flaherty claim that Native Americans, as a rule, chose ecotones for places to settle in: that is, they moved to the coasts of seas and lakes, riverbanks, and meeting points between forested and open areas. [2] For coastal territories are abundant not only in molluscs and fish, but also in coastal birds and their eggs, turtle eggs, crabs, and many other organisms, as well as berries in surrounding forests. Rocky shores may seem inaccessible, but they serve as shelter for many species. Birds nest in cliffs and inhabitants both of the Scottish island of St. Kilda (the most isolated area of the British Isles) and of Tierra del Fuego have specialised in hunting for them.

A common example of hunter-gatherers are the Hadza people, who live on the savannah, and the southern African so-called Bushmen (speakers of languages from the Khoi-San family, who are currently differentiated by use of their own names, for instance !Kung, Ju/'hoansi, /Gui, //Gana, Tyuna where the special characters signify sounds unique to their languages). Meanwhile, among groups that have, until recently, had a hunter-gatherer way of life, many are coastal societies: the Inuits (who used to be called Eskimos) from the Arctic, Sea Gypsies (the Moken) from the coasts of Burma, Thailand and Malaysia, as well as indigenous Andaman Islanders (from an area between India and the Malay Peninsula). Coastal regions were always the most attractive places to live, so often their indigenous inhabitants and their primitive cultures were exterminated and replaced by larger communities and then countries. It's true that cities were first created as a result of the invention

---

[2] Turner N., Davidson-Hunt I., O'Flaherty J. 2003. Living on the Edge: Ecological and Cultural Edges as Sources of Diversity for Social-Ecological Resilience. *Human Ecology*, 31:3

of farming, but the first large villages and settlements belonged to hunter-gatherers on coastal territories. Of all Native Americans, those from the Pacific coast probably pursued activities most similar to modern art, thanks to the plenitude of available seafood, such as large shoals of salmon making their way from the ocean to the rivers of the Rocky Mountains. Their 'close' neighbours from the east of the mountain range, which divided them from the ocean, were largely dispersed and constantly on the move after scant game, rhizomes, and pine seeds.

Winter

When I attempted to periodically live as a wild human in Carpathian forests, I was deeply affected by the issue of climate. For 3-4 months, between November and April, there is snow on the ground and most years, the temperature drops to lower than -20°C for a few days. Frost as well as ground frost are common. Even in the summer, nights are cold and the humid climate and cold dew in the morning enhance the sensation of summer chill. A few years ago, shivering with cold in a shelter I had built from branches and grass, sooty with smoke from the bonfire, sometimes nearly to the point of sickness, still cold despite wearing a warm coat and it being only -3°C outside, I began wondering whether there's any point leading a natural life in this climate. My ancestors travelled from the highlands of Eastern Africa 100 thousand years ago and only reached places where it snows from time to time maybe around 50 or 20 thousand years ago. What's the point of searching for nature in a coat made in a Chinese factory, or even a sheepskin coat made from a sheep I killed myself? Maybe I should be sitting in this shelter naked, even though it's winter? Should I try to build up my stamina? Of course, that would increase my need for food and shock my neighbours as they drive wood out of the forest. The human body has a great capacity for adaptation. Charles Darwin, during his famous trip on the Beagle, observed the indigenous peoples of Tierra del Fuego who lived naked in a temperature close to zero. They didn't know clothes. He even describes snowflakes falling on a breastfeeding woman.

Not only the indigenous inhabitants of Tierra del Fuego were great at dealing with cold weather. Native inhabitants of Australia, who didn't wear clothes, were also forced to heat themselves with their own bodies or the bodies of their dogs on cold nights in the desert. Or, without searching too far, my friend J., who used to live in a lonely cottage on the Subcarpathian periphery, who lives today in a no less wild hamlet in the Lower Beskids, has spent many years barely lighting his stove. In Kopytowa, he slept in a sleeping bag with his dog. Now his dog is dead, so I guess he sleeps alone. Guests who make it to his hut in the winter last about 15 minutes, or an hour if their host offers them one of his homemade spirits.

Tolerance for low temperatures is a question of getting used to them. I left for tropical Thailand in December and returned before the New Year. Three weeks were enough to make me completely unaccustomed to winter. My first outing in the temperature of -3°C seemed like a death sentence, the cold around me prickling my skin. After two weeks in this temperature I can easily spend five minutes in my garden wearing only a jumper.

27

Adaptation to cold can also be observed in the outdoor workshops I run in spring. I organise them between April and May, when temperatures are around 10-20°C but sometimes drop to -3° or -4°C at night. Although not everyone has warm sleeping bags, few people complain about the cold. I once slept under three blankets in the open air at -3°C, because I gave my sleeping bag to my daughter. It was freezing, but I didn't get a cold. During autumn workshops, in mid-September, the temperature at night is around 0°, 5° C and seems lethal, and most conversations revolve around the cold. The difference lies in the fact that in autumn the cold is only just coming, while by spring, after six months of low temperatures, bodies are toughened up.

The British are another example of toughness. Britain is famous for its cold houses. Temperatures in this country in the winter usually range between 5° and 10°C. There is sometimes ground frost at night but frost during the day is limited to a day or two each year. English houses, however, tend to be really cold inside. The British love to save on heating, without leaving even a single room warm, perhaps with the exception of the room in which they have an occasionally used fireplace. Central heating has a clock and is switched on for the morning and the evening. It's completely normal for it to be 15-16° inside and sometimes even less at night. It's much warmer in houses in Poland and Russia. Despite extreme frost, it can be like a sauna indoors. Even those who save on heating usually have at least one room to keep warm in, or an electric or gas heater. In their flats, people usually spend the winter in a temperature of 24-25°C. That's nearly tropical! Where does this difference come from? I think it's because it's harder to get really cold in Britain. Just a little heating and a couple of jumpers are enough to vegetate and spend the winter shivering, but there's no danger of death involved. In the east and north of Europe winter is a serious matter and the freezing cold can cause death. People are prepared: they have their coats, furs, hats, pants, and effective stoves. They use these as much as possible, as much as they can afford to, in order to invert the extreme temperature outside. And so from childhood, they are used to sleeping in warmth, or at least under a warm cover. Small children are warmly dressed and carefully covered at night. In England, children sleep in 15°C under a thin blanket. Small Scottish children still go to school in shorts or skirts, even in the winter. It seems that, like primitive humans, they naturally build up a physiological resistance to cold. The science of human biological development has described many examples of how the natural environment you grow up in has a lifelong effect on your physiological characteristics. For example, the chests of people from high-altitude territories have a larger volume in proportion to their bodies than other people do.[3] We ought to assume that the physiology of the British is also permanently affected by their cold upbringing. Of course we can try to toughen up later in life. A German I met at the *Big Green Gathering* eco-festival told me that he has been living in a tipi for a few years now (in Great Britain, not Germany, where temperatures are more often freezing). It took him many months to really get used to the cold, but it doesn't bother him anymore.

---

[3] Wolański, N. 2006. *Rozwój biologiczny człowieka*. Warszawa: Wydawnictwo Naukowe PWN.

Clothes and heating are the parts of civilization that we get rid of last when trying to live a 'wild' life. We take great pleasure in trying to hunt like the wild, to build shelters, or to create animistic rituals, but it's hard to get rid of our sleeping bag, especially if it cannot be replaced with animal fur. So what's left to us? Digging ourselves into a haystack, warming up by the fire, snuggling up with other people.

Mushroom pickers

Mushroom picking is the last and strongest trace of the hunter-gatherer lifestyle in Poland. Few people collect medicinal plants, and fruit-picking for jams and juices, after an intense XX-century craze, has declined as a result of an increase in the standard of living, due to which people prefer to buy cheap jams and juices in supermarkets. Wild fruits are picked, though rarely, by children who eat them raw, as well as by a handful of enthusiasts. But when it comes to mushrooms, it's very different. Not everyone picks them, but a large percentage of the Polish population, maybe a quarter, devote themselves to this activity with delight and go mushroom picking at least once a year.

Mushroom picking is very different from picking fruit. I think anyone confronted with a choice of going mushroom- or fruit-picking will choose the former. There's little novelty in picking fruit. Every strawberry or blueberry is nearly identical. Picking fruit, if there's plenty of it, is like repeating a mantra. Mushroom picking is like a game of hare and hounds or a treasure hunt. Mushrooms appear only from time to time in particular spots that have to be

30

discovered. Apparently, people most like to play games in which the role of chance is balanced with that of skill and logic. This is the case for mushroom picking. Knowing where to find birch boletes (in grass, surrounded by birch and aspen trees), boletes (in old tree groves, often on sunny hills), slippery jacks (in young pine and larch forests), saffron milk caps (in fir, pine, and spruce marshes), is worth as much as luck and perseverance. And a certain sixth sense for mushrooms is also handy. To be a good mushroom picker, you have to be a keen observer, walker, and clairvoyant.

People also seem to be in awe of the diversity of shapes mushrooms can come in. Not only are species different from each other, but within one species, specimens can be slim and bulgy, straight and crooked, big and small.

Nations differ in their approach to mushrooms. The anthropologist Gordon Wasson introduced the now traditional distinction between mycophilic and mycophobic nations.[4] Mycophiles like and value mushrooms, enjoy picking or growing them, and they aren't afraid of them. Mushrooms are an important part of the culture of countries such as Poland, Russia, China, Mexico, or Italy. They are, on the whole, seldom used by Germanic nations. The English, who associate them mostly with something poisonous, demonic, and dangerous, have tended to avoid them the most. The English language lacks common names of mushrooms and people can identify few of their species. Meanwhile, the average ten-year-old villager in Poland or Russia can identify a few or a dozen edible species. It's

---

[4] Wasson, R.G. 1957. Seeking the magic mushroom. *Life*, 42:100-120.

mostly inedible species, such as the fly agaric or some other toadstools, which appear in illustrated children's books in English. In Polish books, the fly agaric is usually accompanied by the boletus and other edible mushrooms, such as field mushrooms and chanterelles.

Mushrooms are not particularly rich in nutrients. They contain mostly water. They're like food in *Mister Blot's Academy*[5]: magically blown up food that doesn't fill you up. They make a great example of the Indian Maya – illusion. They contain large amounts of chitin, which, like fibre, we cannot digest. Some, such as chanterelles, give us no energy whatsoever, while others, such as the *Boletaceae* family, especially ceps, contain some protein and fat, which were important for the sustenance of underfed peasants. Mushrooms are rich in microelements. It is widely believed among the Chinese that it is healthy to regularly eat small quantities of mushrooms. The clairvoyant Czesław Klimuszko believed that mushrooms have a good effect on the nervous system. Recently there has been increasing evidence for the claim that eating mushrooms stimulates the immune system. On the other hand, mushrooms are more treacherous than plants. Some poisonous mushrooms, such as the death cap *Amanita phalloides* or the raw bay bolete *Imleria badia*, are not bitter in taste. Mushrooms appear in the forest out of nowhere, from underground. They grow at night, are slimy, their toadstools often appearing during full moon, and are associated with witchcraft.

From the available literature, it seems to me that primitive peoples were also divided on the matter and had

---

[5] A film based on a Polish children's novel by Jan Brzechwa (1946).

diverse approaches to edible mushrooms. Native Americans used mushrooms in their cooking to varying degrees, but in general mushrooms were not an important part of their cuisine. The hallucinogenic, 'magic powers' of the fly agaric *Amanita muscaria* were seldom used in North America, in stark contrast to Siberia, where this mushroom played a very important, culture-forming role.

Mushrooms, then, are not an essential part of our diet, but a kind of choice, an option. They have nevertheless been present in forest-inhabiting cultures since prehistoric times. And desert truffles are eaten by the Kalahari hunter-gatherers.

Mushroom-picking technology from the XXI century is no different from the technology used by a hunter-gatherer. It's a pure form of gathering many different species at once. The whole joy of surprise, mystery, of the mini-hunt, is there. Every autumn, millions of Poles are driven to the forest by some atavistic force – an instinct for gathering. Not out of hunger, seldom for gain. Sometimes it even touches those who don't eat mushrooms. Mushroom picking is one big adventure game.

There are few attractions in the small Carpathian village I live in. Besides alcohol, occasional sex with a neighbour, and hunting, mushroom picking is the sole and main pastime of the villagers. Everyone brags about their finds. They carry their basket or bag with them down the street. First they tell you how many proper boletes they've found, then how many saffron milk caps, chanterelles, bay boletes, birch boletes, and finally slippery jacks. Sometimes they find an odd parasol mushroom. The practice begs for a scoring system. We played this game once at my workshops. Boletes and parasol mushrooms were worth five points, saffron milk caps and bay boletes three, birch boletes two, slippery jacks and minor (for instance the amethyst deceiver *Laccaria amethystina*) or less prized mushrooms (like the blusher *Amanita rubescens*) – one point. It was a terrific game and my little daughter Nasim made handwritten certificates for the contestants. There were only a few arguments about whether to count slightly worm-eaten ones, because the completely worm-eaten ones were disqualified from the start. It's a shame that the winner was usually determined by the rare find of some barely edible species. Maybe the point system needs refining?

Other living organisms can also be part of the game. Back when I was a biology student, we had to collect a set of around thirty taxa of a variety of aquatic animals to pass our summer course on invertebrates in the Mazury region. The specifications were fairly precise, and contained, for example: three species of leeches, four species of snails, one sponge, etc. While other students waded up to their waist in mud, I collected only one species, the horse-leech, which I slowly managed to swap around for 30 other taxa. I would gather what was left behind by others, my system being: I'll give you a leech that you don't have, and you give me two stoneflies. It was a primitive business of sorts.

In Rzepnik, my village, mushrooms have another layer of meaning. They have replaced the term 'good morning'. Or maybe it never really existed here. Locals don't knock on the door, ring the bell, say 'good morning' or 'goodbye'. They go straight for the door, pushing it with all their force, even if it's closed, hoping that the lock will give under the pressure of their body. They tug the handle and when they're leaving, they just get up and start walking without a word. Those originally deported from the other

34

side of the river Bug, who settled in this region after World War II, who seem to have more manners, are an exception. But let's not be fooled. The phrases 'good morning', or even 'how are you', are supplanted for the summer and autumn months by the question 'Any mushrooms?', and its answer, depending on the state of the forest: 'yes', 'no', or 'yes, but all wormy'. There's always hope for mushrooms, because it's always either before full moon or after, before new moon or after new moon. It's just those worms. They're the worst.

Natural sex

What does 'natural sex' mean? What sort of sex did the average primitive have? Different anthropologists and ethnographers provide all sorts of answers. I personally think that its main characteristic was brevity. There were no guidebooks on how to please a woman, and Tantric and Taoist inventions, while ancient, are advanced human achievements. Talayesva, a Native American from the Hopi tribe, the main character of *Sun Chief*, claimed that warriors from his tribe would have fast intercourse, without any delay, giving in to their drive.[6]

Talayesva also describes another Hopi concept. To be pure in anticipation of a religious ceremony, a man has to abstain from sex for four days. This resembles Jewish beliefs – a man is impure on a day in which he has had sex or ejaculated. In Catholicism and Buddhism, the concept of

---

[6] Simmons, L.W. (ed.) 1942. *Sun Chief: the autobiography of a Hopi Indian*. New Haven.

celibacy is extreme – priests and monks have to abstain from sex entirely. Does it not seem more natural to abstain from it from time to time? In hunter-gatherer societies, as a rule, shamans have families and celibate castes only began to occur in civilizations which introduced division of labour between the sexes.

Seeing a naked and attractive person that we have a physical desire for, we have no doubt that this lust and drive is primal and common to all animals. But how much is what happens next dictated or altered by our culture? Even a kiss is a matter of culture, not nature – in some societies, kissing doesn't exist! Are there any societies in which people don't insert penises into vaginas? I haven't found one yet, but maybe there are? Maybe there were even tribes in which children were conceived through a shower made out of the sperm of all the men in it, who ejaculated by themselves (or with one another's help) into a coconut shell. A bit of a lottery. When I was in my teens, my friend asked me: 'How did they think of putting the penis in the hole? Who thought of it? Who invented it?'. It's true that in puritanical communist China (and not only there) there were cases of couples who didn't know they had to 'put it in' undergoing infertility treatment. Then again, isn't it complicated! Wouldn't it be easier to be a fish? They knock against each other in their shoals, pouring sperm onto eggs which slowly fall down onto the distant seabed...

Is masturbation natural? Current theoreticians of sex think it is. The Egyptian God Ra apparently created the world from a solitary ejaculation... Meanwhile Bronisław Malinowski, in his studies of Trobriand sexuality, notes that they consider masturbation to be sad and weird. After all, there's always someone else keen to join in.

Moken

The Surin Islands are one of the most beautiful places in the world. They are made up of small islands surrounded by coral reefs, a few dozen miles west from the shores of Thailand. The Andaman Sea was brought attention to by the tsunami in 2004. On the other side of the Andaman Sea lie the Andaman Islands with their last relics of hunter-gatherers – the half-naked native inhabitants of these islands hiding in the shade of the tropical jungle. Here, on the eastern side of this sea, lives a completely different group of hunter-gatherers. The Moken, also called the Chao Ley, don't look stereotypically wild, compared to primitive Andamans. In handmade boats and clothes bought or received from others, they have been wandering around the Sunda Islands the islands of the Andaman Sea for centuries, from Burma to Indonesia. The world found out about them after the tsunami, when they lost their boats but survived mainly thanks to their observational skills. Some of them, up to 2004, never bought rice, despite its importance to Asian cultures. They lived on fish, molluscs, prawns, and wild fruit and vegetables. Some families from this group have already undergone a deep transformation. They are now settled in villages built by various companies or on their own, living to a lesser extent on fish, and more off tourism or trade.

In Thailand, the most independent Moken live on the Surin Islands. I arrive on this island, where the national park is located, as a normal tourist on a motor boat, and snorkel to take a look at stunning coral reefs while I'm there. Then I walk around the island. It's covered in equatorial forest. The

Islands look like inaccessible oval domes. The coast is mostly rocky, hard to reach, but also full of mussels and sea snails which make for wonderful food. I don't get to the village-port of Moken itself. Because of the rising wave, we sail past the village (which I can see from a distance) and return to Kurraburi. I start to feel sick. I keep my head over a plastic bag after swallowing two motion sickness tablets. I meet the Moken themselves on the beach of the national park, where they have anchored a few boats. They are very dark-skinned compared to the Thai. A few men and boys are sitting in their boats. The women, according to our guidebooks, work as cleaning ladies for the national park.

The list

In many chapters of this book I try to make sense of what is wild and what is not, what is natural and what is not. Looking at this in depth, we can begin to see that many things are far from obvious, for example, whether it is more natural to base one's diet largely on meat (like hunter-gatherers), or to return to the sustenance of apes – fruit and leaves. Or whether our beginning was on the savannah or on the coast.

But maybe we should reverse our way of thinking and consider what is unnatural.

Trainers? I guess our tropical forefathers didn't wear them. As I write this, I'm sitting in a restaurant in the Thai jungle and I can see that even now, flip-flops and all sorts of sandals are dominant here, feet are bare, tanned, 'aware', aired. Footwear is a necessity in cold climates. For instance, it would be hard for the first inhabitants of North America to survive without leather moccasins or fur-lined winter boots. But footwear also became a habitat for fungi.

Clothes? Trainers are also clothes, so I guess I could say the same here: the more tropical, the more natural. The problem is that now, even in the tropics, people usually cover a large part of their bodies, even though they often walk barefoot or in flip-flops. But if we look to Amazonian tribes or the more isolated inhabitants of Africa, we can see more nudity there.

Phones? Phones and the Internet are not natural. The amount of stimuli and the ease with which we can access information make us feel swamped with data, proposals, signals, temptations. On the other hand, the sense it gives us of living in one global village brings us closer together and makes the world shrink. McLuhan wrote a lot on this before the Internet was even invented.

Cars? Yes, they are the work of the devil. False materials. Imported fuels, travelling too fast, too many costs, a deceptive sense of freedom, total isolation from one's surroundings.

The examples go on. Only our bodies, our loved ones, and nature remain stripped of technology, as do nature's forces, species, and most simple tools: the stick and the stone (without counting coconut shells, but that's a local bonus).

Complete sterility

Does wild mean dirty? Full of bacteria and worms? Shat on? Torn? That's how the inhabitants of Europe used to imagine 'savages'. They pictured them as dirtier than themselves but they were usually wrong. The concept of cleanliness is relative. Many different taboos prevent the spreading of illnesses and pathogens and are often different for reasons to do with climate or historical conditioning of diseases. Europe in the early Middle Ages was not only, as it remained later on, dirty, but also relaxed. People were not ashamed of their nudity, members of both sexes washed together, and prostitutes had sex with their clients in public baths. Still, epidemics of cholera and syphilis and more minor illnesses did separate people from each other. In expanding cities, contact with another human being meant danger. Clothing and limiting of physical touch were a great preventative measure. And so now we wear clothes and use forks and condoms.

The widespread Eastern European perception of Muslims from the Middle East as dirty seems especially insulting. Islam commands washing, even of the earlobes, five times a day before prayer. Their use of water rather than paper to wash themselves after defecation and frequent use of steam rooms makes many Muslims the cleanest people in the world. However, it is true that in some parts of the Middle East, the level of cleanliness of the surroundings is lower, but this reflects their different perception of public space, and, above all, simply their poverty.

The wild seems dirty but isn't always so. A carpet in a modern home contains more pathogenic organisms than the floor of a beech wood. In the forest, there's a balance between different species of fungi and plants which are lethal to other species. Indoors, this balance is less stable. Something that might seem clean might sometimes be clean and other times be full of germs making use of this biological wasteland. They wouldn't have survived in a forest teeming with life. A large part of our body mass consists of bacteria that live in our organism. By definition, we cannot be sterile. To be sterile is to be dead.

Of course, it's good to have a moderate approach to keeping things clean. There's an optimal amount of bacteria that allows for a fairly healthy life – probably the amount required can be found in a not-particularly-clean country house or in the forest, while there are too few in a supermarket or a chemist's and too many in a heap of dung, a town marketplace or the waiting room in a medical practice.

Naturalness and gnosis

Thinking about naturalness and wildness brings us to another subject: tradition. On one hand, we can treat a return to nature as a return to the 'traditions of our ancestors' such as neopagans, proponents of a return to shamanism or Slavic or Germanic religions. On the other hand, it could mean turning our backs on traditions and customs, which is strictly speaking impossible to do (language itself is a product of tradition, a collective good). However, the idea itself is worthy of exploration.

What should people who don't want to return to nature by reading survival guides and books on shamanism do? By reading these, we can find out how to light a fire, build a shelter, hunt, or enter different states of consciousness through 'primitive techniques'. In the long run, there's no point in discarding everything and starting from scratch, because even in a friendly climate and environment, this would require working on for generations. Still, in some cases the 'getting rid of everything' game, the search for a mute message in nature and deep within ourselves is great fun. It's a great way of exploring the world. I built my first shelter made of grass and branches without following any instructions. I had seen tipis made of fabric that are often built by admirers of the cultures of the Plains Indians, and it always made me wonder what they would do if they couldn't purchase the fabrics. Would they hunt? For what? Bison? Aurochs? Deer (whose skins are smaller)? Eureka! They'd use dry grass! And so I began to assemble a tipi out of sticks and then cover it with hand-picked long grass. Other than through films I watched as a child, I received no instruction on how to build a shelter. But once I got good at building them (good enough for them to shelter me from rain), I began to notice exactly the same shelters in different books – survival guidebooks, an ethnographic atlas of Siberia, on websites about Bushmen or in a chapter on Apache architecture. A model revealed repeatedly.

The idea to put a larger number of such shelters in a circle seems equally natural to the idea of building one in the first place. That's how we end up with a village.

I think that a lot of things need to be rediscovered simply by living in conditions a little closer to the primitive – in the forest, in a shelter, under some small roof. Eating mostly what's right in front of us. We could create a new culture. We could change the names of the months. All sorts of names that are not in use at the moment, such as the month of the anemone, cuckooing of cuckoos, or the month of blooming elderflower, spring to mind. When you sleep under the stars, you notice the effect of moon cycles without the use of biodynamic calendars. You also acknowledge the power of the elements: water, fire, earth, air, maybe also, following the Chinese, wood and metal.

Body painting, smearing oneself with mud, blood, charcoal, or plant juices, suggests itself much faster than clothing.

Just take a look at children's games, especially when they play 'Indians', and you will see how much creativity and unused ideas even the smallest human head is teeming with. We do have to be careful and remember that even children can be cruel. When I recall my own or my friends' ideas, such as tying someone to a tree next to an anthill or a competition involving throwing stones at cars (who'll kill the driver first?), they send a shiver down my spine.

Return to nature and the tipi

I know many people for whom the tipi has become a symbol of a return to nature. The word 'tipi' comes from the language of one of the Plains Indians tribes, the Lakota. It was used to describe a cone-shaped shelter constructed with long, thin perches, covered with skins or canvas, which served as a household to many Plains Indians. Many bison skins are required for the making of one tipi, but it's a very spacious shelter. A tipi of five or six metres in length fits dozens of people around the fire. A tipi is portable and authentically nomadic. It both gives the sense of being 'at home', shade, protection from wind, and privacy. Like most primitive shelters, the tipi has many shortcomings – it's easy to break into and is quickly subject to wear and tear. If its poles are not completely even, some rainwater usually makes its way inside, which makes life inside it much more difficult (poles for Native American tipis were made out of a particular species of pine tree and were very thin and straight...). Tipis aren't especially warm either. It's difficult to keep warm inside them during the winter without constantly adding to the fire.

Tipi-style shelters were built not only by the Plains Indians, but also by many northern tribes in Canada as well as in Siberia. The northern tipis were usually lower and flatter. The tall Plains tipi gets rid of smoke and rainwater fast but it is a waste of skins. It's also harder to keep such a large space warm, so people of the North tended to nest together in small, low shelters, in heavy smoke.

Being primitive isn't always pleasant. Smoke is carcinogenic. This wasn't a concern for primitive people, who often lived to about thirty or forty, but it's a thing worth remembering. There are many carcinogenic substances in nature. It's a lie that only humans produce them. Common bracken (*Pteridium aquilinum*), the sprouts of which are eaten by the Chinese and the Japanese, and which also used to be consumed by Native Americans, is also carcinogenic. Betel, chewed as a stimulant by the inhabitants of South Asia, is also carcinogenic, as is even our hogweed, which was used for food in Poland.

Why has the tipi become so popular among contemporary lovers of nature? Well, I think its popularity rose together with the popularisation of the car. A tipi is large and heavy. You can't fit it in your backpack. You can, however, throw it into a van. We associate a tipi with the Plains Indians, and those in turn with freedom, chivalry, wildness. A tipi is attractive and big. A few tipis in a circle look monumental. A tipi of five or seven metres in diameter is like a large living room that allows for many people to assemble in it, and is a space akin to our flats, rather than a den like a tent or a wigwam.

Is a tipi – and I mean the kind of tipi that's covered with factory-made canvas – natural? Not in its construction. At least the poles are cut out of real trees. It is, however, 'more' natural in its function. It encourages a nomadic lifestyle, closer to the elements of air, fire, and water.

Bamboo

Bamboo is, along with the banana, another (sub)tropical miracle of nature. Both are perennial with a distinct geometry. In some parts of Asia it's a common, often basic building material. At the same time, it symbolises beauty. I first confronted bamboo in its natural habitat in Thailand. In the south of this country lies the large Khaosok National Park which, along with a few adjacent stretches of forest, forms one of the biggest protected forest areas in Southeast Asia. The presence of this fairly natural forest, within reach of the main road, attracts tourists interested in nature. Of course, I mean gibbons and tigers, not girls in Bangkok clubs. It's partly a virgin forest, because it grows on limestone rocks which are difficult to access. In other places, it has been affected by people. The presence of a large amount of gigantic bamboo, yet to reach its original size, is a sign of this.

During my first walk through this village, smaller than but very similar to Białowieża (the mini-town near the wildest forest in Europe), thanks to the national park and the guides around it, as well as to a kind of isolation, being surrounded by the forest and its presence, together with a tourist bar subculture (about a dozen of small restaurants and guesthouses), we were hassled by various guides offering all sorts of 'trips' and 'trekkings' – boat rides on the lake, rafting, exploring caves, or searching for the largest flower in the world, the rafflesia, which grows there.

They all had different nicknames, such as 'Jungle Man' or some other jungly thing like the real Jungle Guy. Some of these offers seemed kitsch. Some guy suggested walking around the forest and bamboo cooking, 'bamboo cookeeng', with the accent falling on the 'eeng'. I did want to spend the night in the jungle. I was not particularly scared but I didn't want to sleep on the ground, I didn't have a hammock, and besides, I thought that maybe there was something more contained in this simple offer. I made an arrangement with a nice guy who spoke some English. We left within a day, we wandered around the forest, set up camp, he made some of his 'bambu kukiing' and we went back the following day. I didn't make any hunting suggestions, as, after all, we were in a National Park. So my guide took all sorts of curry accessories and a machete with him. After a few hours of wandering, he pointed to a spot in the forest, by the river, and we set camp. He hung my hammock up right next to the fire. 'No, thank you'. 'I don't wanna burn' – I added in Polish. Lyng – that's his name – carved a full tea set with his machete within 10 minutes and with great precision: there were mugs, a spoon, and some tubes that looked like they belonged to a church organ. He cooked dinner in these pipes. Bamboo shoots have a pouch every few dozen centimetres, which allows for them to be easily transformed into vessels. The pipes lean against a bar hung up from two vertical sticks. The fire lashes against them, so of course these are only single-use vessels. It's a simple thing, but Lyng pouring his meals into halves of a trough split lengthways pleased the eye and we seemed to dine like kings on a meal that was, of course, very spicy. Eating his soup, I become more and more hungry. I tried to explain that I thought it would be nice to eat something wild: I found large fruits that looked like unripe apples. A tree with red bark and large dark leaves (*Dillenia indica*). 'Good'? I asked. 'Very good' – Lyng replied. He cut off a slice. I tried. It was horrible, bitter, sour, and hard. 'Very good with this' and he mixes chilli with salt. 'Yes, better' – I add. I guess even dung tastes interesting with chilli and salt. I went into the water. Hundreds of fishes swam away but soon came back. A dozen of them pinched my feet. I tried to catch one. 'Hee, hee, hee'. Lyng plunged into the water and shortly swam back up with two. In an attempt to take a look at them, they wiggled out of my hand. I spent an hour making all sorts of bridges, putting bamboo sticks in the water. Maybe that would have tempted them? Nothing. Lyng said: 'No problem' and took out a hook and a fishing rod. He speared a piece of our dinner onto it and I cast the line. I kept casting and casting but nothing happened. 'Wait, no problem'. We left a trap and walked off. 'Now trekking animal, good time'. We spent a good two hours powering through the jungle and only spotted a few spiders and a stick insect. Moments after our return, a twenty-centimetre-long bullhead took our bait. I threw myself at it, wanting to touch it. 'No touch, poison'. He showed me that it had some sort of poisonous spike. I looked it in the eyes. It had large coral eyes like a teddy bear. It breathed heavily with its gills. I touched my stomach. I was quite full but a bullhead like this will taste great grilled. I looked it in the eyes, I looked at its gills, and then remember the story about the fisherman and his wife. I asked it to grant my wish that things never get worse for me than they were then and let it out. Splash. Lyng didn't give up. He said: 'Too small'. He cast again. After five minutes he had a similar one, slightly larger. I took it in my hand and threw it in the water. I ate it virtually. I forgot to make another wish: 'Let me come back here again'.

Pedro and Weronika

My friend Pedro comes from a certain Western European country. He's nearly two metres tall with long, fair hair and a beaming smile on his face. Over ten years ago, he came to the Polish mountains and fell in love with them. He felt that it's here that he will be able to find 'his' way of returning to the natural world. I am writing about him because he is the perfect character for this book. He uses the word 'natural' all the time. The walls of the caravan he lives in are filled not with mineral wool, but are, as he says, 'natural', made with sawdust and lime. His clothes are also natural – he wears a linen suit and a felt hat. Pedro worships nature. He didn't want to live in an unnatural home. He spent many years living in a tipi in this Carpathian valley. Not all the time, but he did spend many months there, even in the winter. His guests were always shocked by his resistance to cold. A small pile of firewood was enough for him, allowing him to make some tea, but the odd visitor would shiver with cold...

Pedro doesn't kill animals and is vegetarian. He believes that he will be able to survive here from nature, from wild fruit and the vegetables he grows. For now, he eats rice and other grains that he buys in the local shop. A few years ago, he told me that all you need to do to get veg to grow is to make a ball out of seeds of different plants and manure and throw them around. The veg will then grow on its own. I'm not sure whether he did that, but I don't believe in such a miraculous method of spreading food.

Pedro, like most people in search of nature, like me, lives in a state of constant self-contradiction. He runs away from the world of Babylon, into the wilderness, where he selects elements of a wild way of life that he's missed… the shelter, the silence, the stream. He accepts other aspects of civilisation, but with a minimalistic approach. After all, he doesn't have electricity.. He does, however, own a chainsaw and a laptop, which he charges in a nearby village. A few years ago he didn't allow trees to be cut down – everything had to be done by hand – but nowadays, he finds himself forced to make things a little simpler.

Pedro is still a mystic. Although he has so much in common with the civilization he hates, he is far ahead compared to most people. He has survived for a long time in extreme conditions while remaining drawn to and warm towards others. He found a partner who wants to live like him and started a family. They are raising two children without electricity but with a laptop. Without a house but in a warm caravan by the rippling woodland stream.

I'm curious about his fate but I trust he will maintain his wonderful, 'natural' part of himself. I'm grateful to him for showing me a certain amazing appliance. This was a long time ago, when no-one had heard of USB sticks yet, and I certainly hadn't. Pedro, as a nomad, wore one around his neck together with some amulet. He had everything on

49

it, all of his files. He forgot it at my house once. He left it on my desk. I stupidly thought it was some kind of amulet, a piece of some archaic electrical appliance. When he visited me again, he shouted 'it's at yours that I left that USB stick!'.

Interestingly enough, Pedro came to this country on foot. As a member of a nomadic carpenters' guild he was forced to make his journey without a car. As the Germans say, *langsam fahren, lange fahren.*

A year after writing these words, I told Pedro and his wife Weronika about what I'm writing here. Weronika protested: 'What about me? It's true Pedro got here first, but it's me who carries branches from the forest, cooks, and does the washing in cold stream water!'. I'm sorry, Weronika! I dedicate this chapter to the two of you but out of sheer laziness I'm not going to change the pronouns...

I'm now writing the English translation of this book exactly ten years after the original Polish version. The couple have split up, but they still live not far from each other in the same mountains. When I go back to stories of real people who inspired me to write this book, they are all still living in accord with their own twisted idea of what is natural. They pick things which suit them. They persist and stay close to nature, even with their cars and laptops. Sometimes a little compromise goes a long way.

Waldek

Waldek lives just across the stream from Pedro. They're the only people in this deserted area. Waldek is also looking for a way to get back to nature here. He has a log cabin, a horse and a cow, maybe even a goat – I can't remember, we don't know each other well enough. He doesn't have electricity. He's nearly self-sufficient, at least according to local legend. He sows something or other, cultivates the land and produces milk. He works like a real farmer. He has reached the perfect independence many seek in vain. In terms of how much he's cut himself off from the world, he's ahead of everyone. His independence has reached the limit. He's annoyed by hippies, lost tourists, and even old friends who visit from time to time. He should officially be called a hermit. After all, what's all this for, just for himself? That way at least they'll name him a saint and he'll set an example for other people.

Journey

As I write these words, I am flying above southern Asia. The plane has left Phuket in the south of Thailand and is racing over the Indian Ocean. We've passed one of the Andaman Islands, cut across India, Pakistan, Afghanistan, the Caspian Sea, and will eventually land in Munich.

Is travelling natural? Did primitive people travel? How far? After all, they were nomads...

The word 'nomad' invokes associations with someone who is swept by fate from country to country. But as archaeological and anthropological data shows, most journeys made by primitive nomads were more like orbiting around their family land, where the bones or ashes of their ancestors rested, where their ghosts lived, where there were plants they knew and collected and animals that they knew how to hunt. Large migrations occurred chiefly through catastrophes, because of madmen, or by accident; through looking for new hunting ground during periods of hunger, or a son in conflict with his father, who would take part of the tribe to wander with him, or because a boat went off its course.

'Air miles' have been in fashion recently. People who take long-haul flights pollute the environment to an awful extent. One flight has the carbon footprint of a year's worth of their commute to work. I look out of the plane window at misty Pakistan. *Mea culpa, mea culpa,* never again.

But how am I supposed to travel? By train, car, motorbike, bicycle, horse? On foot?

In the nineteenth century, a certain Hungarian walked his way around the world. He left Budapest and walked East through Mongolia, then took a boat and walked across America. It took a few years.

My friend cycled from Poland to Siberia. When the situation in the Middle East allows for it, people drive from Western Europe to India or Thailand. My great-grandmother returned from Irkutsk to Poland partly on foot, partly hitching rides on tanks and lorries.

The furthest I've walked in a day is 26 miles – a marathon. I can't take any more. But some can walk up to a hundred. I guess the reach of primitive people was measured in such 26 mile units, equivalent to a day spent walking, a long evening of rest, and a sleep.

From reading about hunter-gatherer tribes, I get the feeling that they can be classified under a few categories. First, of those who moved around in more or less the same kind of environment but often at large distances, wandering after game. For example, the Plains Indians searched for bison. The second category is of those who zigzagged between two kinds of environment with different food available in each and didn't have to travel far to do so, like the indigenous people of the West Coast of North America. For most of the year, they fished salmon and they spent the rest chiefly on gathering wild plants, mostly berries and bulbs in the forests. This was the hunter-gatherer equivalent of settlement and urbaneness. Studies show that larger and more settled groups of hunter-gatherers were concentrated on the coast and in places that were especially rich in food. Inhabitants of places that were monotonous or less rich in food were forced to travel. Finally, the rhythm of travel could be complicated but repetitive. The yearly cycle of Paiute life has been well described by Emma Lou Davis[7]. She writes that Indians from around Mono Lake, at the foot of the Sierra Nevada hills, fed on parts of plants, roots, fruit, the seeds of grasses, larvae of *Hydropyrus hians* ants, caterpillars of *Coloradia pandora*, moths that feed on pine trees, rodents, lizards, rabbits, and occasionally larger game. Their main food in winter was composed of large pine seeds. During winter, the Paiute people would break up into groups and each family would camp alone and choose a pine forest or another warm place along the eastern side of the lake. They would eat mainly provisions (mostly pine seeds) and rodents. In March, they would move to the western side of the lake to bright pine forests, where they hunted for deer and collected young green shoots. Then, at the start of summer, they would move to open fields, especially around the lake, where they would collect seeds,

---

[7] Davis, E.L. 1962. Hunter-gatherers of Mono Lake. *The Masterkey*, 36(1): 23-28.

fruits, and rhizomes. When it was time for collecting ant larvae, which gathered on the shores of the lake, these places looked like one big campsite, with shelters stretching out for miles. Finally, in the autumn they would move to pine forests, where they collected large quantities of pine cones containing pine nuts, and when the harvest was plentiful, they would also overwinter in shelters made of branches with floors slightly dug into the ground.

The Original Affluent Society

The 'original affluent society' is a term coined by the American anthropologist Marshall Sahlins, who first introduced it at the *Man the Hunter* symposium in Chicago in 1966.

The symposium was of great importance. A breakthrough occurred in the way in which the lives of primitive hunter-gatherers were perceived. Until then, they had been associated with poverty, hunger, and primitivism. Then they became associated with a sort of ideal of a 'golden age', because apparently they didn't go hungry, and their spiritual culture was often very elaborate (as were the less visible aspects of their material culture).

Sahlins called the economy of hunter-gatherer societies a 'Zen economy'. Sahlins argues that hunter-gatherers can achieve a sense of affluence by not needing much and by satisfying these basic needs in any way possible.

Sahlins quotes Lorna Marshall, who spent years living among the Basarwa of Botswana:

As the !Kung[8] come into more contact with Europeans and this is already happening - they will feel sharply the lack of our things and will need and want more. It makes them feel inferior to be without clothes when they stand among strangers who are clothed. But in their own life and with their own artifacts they were comparatively free from material pressures. Except for food and water (important exceptions!) of which the Nyae Nyae Kung have a sufficiency - but barely so, judging from the fact that all are thin though not emaciated - they all had what they needed or could make what they needed, for every man can and does make the things that men make and every woman the things that women make... They lived in a kind of material plenty because they adapted the tools of their living to materials which lay in abundance around them and which were free for anyone to take (wood, reeds, bone for weapons and implements, fibres for cordage, grass for shelters). or to materials which were at least sufficient for the needs of the population....[9]

Sahlins pays special attention to the large amount of free time at the hunter-gatherers' disposal. Based on works by McCarthy and McArthur on Arnhem Land and by Richard Lee on the South African !Kung tribe, his view is that hunter-gatherers work only for around twenty hours per week, that is, half the time people work nowadays.

---

[8] The exclamation mark preceding the word Kung signifies a click that doesn't exist in other language families.

[9] Marshall, L. 1961. Sharing, Talking, and Giving: Relief of Social Tensions Among "Kung Bushmen. *Africa,* 31:23149.

And James Woodburn writes about Hadza people:

A woman gathers on one day enough food to feed her family for three days, and spends the rest of her time resting in camp, doing embroidery, visiting other camps, or entertaining visitors from other camps. For each day at home, kitchen routines, such as cooking, nut cracking, collecting firewood, and fetching water, occupy one to three hours of her time. This rhythm of steady work and steady leisure maintained throughout the year. The hunters tend to work more frequently than the women, but their schedule uneven. It 'not unusual' for a man to hunt avidly for a week and then do no hunting at all for two or three weeks. Since hunting is an unpredictable business and subject to magical control, hunters sometimes experience a run of bad luck and stop hunting for a month or longer. During these periods, visiting, entertaining, and especially dancing are the primary activities of men.[10]

Pain

Resistance to pain is one of the least explored human traits. Just as the character in one of Herman Hesse's books says that he can fast, meditate and wait, the primitive human could say: 'I can hunt, gather, fast, and stand pain'. Pain, an inevitable part of every human life, had a stronger

---

[10] Woodburn, J. 1968. An introduction to Hadza Ecology, in: Lee and I. DeVore (eds.), *Man the Hunter*. Chicago: Aldine.

presence in a time without injections, paracetamol, or hospitals. Although humans discovered narcotic substances that helped them to cope with pain, such as opium or some species of nightshades, like henbane or daturas, back in prehistoric times, people's upbringing was geared towards withstanding even extreme pain without complaint. This becomes apparent when we examine the commonplace nature of extremely cruel rites of passage.

One of the cruellest rites of passage was invented by the Aborigines.[11] In many Australian tribes young boys, barely teenagers, would undergo so-called 'subincision', that is, an incision of the penis. A sort of extended version of circumcision. The penis was split lengthwise, like a hot-dog, damaging the vas deferens but leaving the ureters intact. So pee went down normally but semen ran down the root of the penis (which may have played a role in limiting fertility). Of course, it was all very painful. The rite was performed with a sharp stone or a shell, and later with various debris of industrial civilization (glass, for example). Boys would suffer for weeks from wounds that were difficult to heal, and mothers would chew on their sons' foreskin, singing ritual songs.

The study of Plains Indians' rituals delivers riveting descriptions of tolerance to pain. Their initiation rituals, the *vision quest*, Sun Dance and related rituals were all steeped in cruelty. Before embarking on vision-seeking quests, members of the Crow tribe would cleanse themselves in a sweat lodge and climb to the top of a hill, where they would prepare themselves a bed of fir branches. Then they would

---

[11] Szyjewski, A. 2000. *Religie Australii*. Kraków: Nomos.

cut off a part of their fingers to encourage the arrival of spirits and lie there naked, with a cut-off finger, for four days and nights. With no food or drink. And so, on the verge of death, they would receive their visions.

In the XIX century, George Catlin described, in great detail, the cruel rituals of warriors from the Mandan tribe from the upper course of the Missouri. The warriors, to prove their courage or their trust in the Great Spirit, were hung from special, gallows-like structures.

Their skin would be cut in a few places on their bodies and stretched so that the warrior was tied down. Some warriors would go through this ritual a few times in their lives. At the end of the ritual, they would let one of their fingers be cut off. The first time, it would be the little finger of their left hand. The second time, another finger from the left hand, although sometimes the most devoted would let one of the fingers of their right hand be cut off. While describing the bloody rituals of the Mandans, Catlin stresses how well the wounds of the rituals' participants healed. The finger amputations involved a relatively small amount of blood. The wounds were not bandaged and nothing was applied to them.

The African Pygmies, too, had initiation rituals that involved strong pain – boys were whipped while gagged or had their teeth drilled. In central Australia there also existed a ritual of knocking teeth out. And so on.

Smoke

The invention of fire is older than agriculture, shepherding, or metal. It is probably older than humans

58

themselves. Sources show that *Homo erectus* may already have used fire. It isn't certain whether they knew how to start a fire, but they probably kept it going without letting it go out for years on end.

Where there is fire, there is smoke. While humans lived in a hot climate and fire was used only for cooking or keeping wild animals at bay, smoke wasn't a problem. It only became a nuisance in cramped shelters during long winter days. On the one hand, it kept insects away. On the other, it made breathing difficult, was probably one of the only carcinogenic elements of the primitive human's lifestyle and was also detrimental to eye health. Eye diseases caused by smoke were one of those strange ancient ailments that gave way to diseases of civilization, such as cancer, diabetes, and circulatory system diseases.

In Western Europe, where winters are not too extreme, large chimneys and fireplaces spread heat fairly effectively hundreds of years ago. Eastern Europe, however, was home to smoke-filled huts all the way up to the nineteenth and twentieth century. How did it happen? Well, without a chimney, heat took longer to escape from the hut, and the smoke preserved the house walls. Smoke escaped through a hole in the ceiling and then made its way through the thatched roof. When landlords in the XIX century began to demand that peasants build chimneys, the latter thought that their landlords had gone mad because they couldn't understand how you could throw heat out of the house. Nowadays, we're irritated by a small stream of cigarette smoke on a bus stop.

Rainbow Family

At 19, as a result of my 'fast-track' education which involved skipping a few years of schooling due to my unusual, over-active brain, I had just returned from the Białowieża Forest, where I was collecting materials for my Masters dissertation when Krzysiek, my friend from school, showed me pictures from a party that had taken place just an hour away from my hometown of Krosno. It was the Rainbow Family meetup (later in this chapter called R).

Informal R meetups started in 1972 in the United States but after a few years the idea travelled to Europe, where since 1983 every summer a 'European Gathering of the R Family' takes place in some remote location.

R has a lot of hippie traits. It looks like a hippie convention and, in a sense, it is one. But it came into being at the end of that era. The idea of these gatherings is spreading love and brotherhood, undergoing a healing exchange of energy, and to live, at least for a short while, away from Babylon, as participants call the normal, commercial world.

When I saw Krzysiek's photo, I didn't know about any of this. He presented it simply as a gathering of 'ecologists', 'Native American enthusiasts', 'these cool oddballs from the West'. This was the second gathering in a row to be held in Poland. The first took place in the Bieszczady Mountains, this one was close by, in Polany Surowiczne. This was an exception – usually the gatherings are in a different part of Europe every year.

Krzysiek told me about people spitting fire, giving out food for free, smearing themselves in mud, and about girls who walked around naked. I regretted not having been there, so close to home, at R, and spent the next few years trying to find out how to get there. I wasn't in much touch with that circle and the Internet was only just beginning to evolve. When I finally tracked down an R meeting I already know a little more about the ideals behind it, and I myself was nearly thirty with a wife and three year old daughter.

I attended my first R in Croatia. I'm not entirely sure where because the spot was changed at the last minute. We went by car. This was not long after the Yugoslav Wars. On our way, we passed through villages with holes in their walls, dumped fridges and appliances, abandoned homes. The party took place near the Bosnian border, in a beautiful valley called Pagan, which means Saucepan.

Just like Krzysiek told me, R brings to mind not only hippie associations but also Native American ones. It looks like a ritual convention of some tribe. This impression is made stronger by the amount of canvas tipis and all sorts of *ad hoc* wigwams, which render the much more numerous tarpaulin roofs and commercial tents practically invisible.

The connection of R with Native Americans is strong but blurry. It's not like the case of Indianist movements, which were a game of copying Indians, a game at belonging to some specific tribe. I think it's closer to Seton's scouting concept of Indians. There are no plumes in sight, although you can see eagle feathers in amulets from time to time. There are no weapons either, because the gathering is vegan in its ideals. You do see people with painted faces, dressed 'differently', as well as the aforementioned tipis. A lot of people sit and speak 'like' Indians – in a circle, on the ground, with concentration, slowly. Sometimes – though rarely, as it requires a lot of work and most people find it

61

difficult to be intensely active – various ceremonies and workshops take place, for instance the Indian sweat lodge rite (however massage workshops are the most popular).

Of course when I speak of Indians, I mean the Plains Indians, or rather an idealised image of them similar to that of the scouts' or Indianists' that some members of these gatherings copy. To say that something was done 'like the Indians did it' is the highest form of positive rating for it. Sometimes references to other tribes are made, but the most important legend for R is the prophecy of the chief of the Hopi tribe (apparently it's made up, but it's really beautiful nevertheless).

Food at R is free. Twice a day, a 'food circle' is formed. In the centre of the gathering, where four 'Indian' colourful flags signifying the four directions hang, people gather round in a circle and the food is brought in massive saucepans and offered out by volunteers. The food is quite simple – it's usually some kind of soup, flatbread, and fruit. Vegan. Unsalted. Often burnt, because it's cooked by chatty volunteers. Besides, when you're cooking for a few thousand people, accidents happen. I once made a thousand flatbreads myself.

Once, while dicing courgettes that could fill a whole tractor trailer, I witnessed an awful fight. It's a rare thing at R, where everyone tries to stay stylish, chilled, with a sense of distance, and to maintain a 'love attitude' and 'non-violence'. A participant was caught adding salt to the soup, while for many people in the kitchen, salt was an enemy. She was then just about verbally lynched and in the evening the circle had a large discussion over whether to add salt to dishes or not.

Listening to arguments from either side, I began to wonder what my idealised Primitive Human would have to say (there's no idealised Indian or Aborigine in my head – I have, rather, an Idealised General Primitive Human of the Temperate Forest). Many societies that formed far away from the sea, such as the South American Yanomami, had no salt and didn't use it, but their bodies functioned perfectly well thanks to the mineral salts contained in meat, vegetables, and ash from the fire, which their food was contaminated with. However, the presence of salt is natural to people from coastal regions. Wild maritime vegetables, for example wild beets from the coast of England (which are well worth trying) are very salty. Just eating them supplies us with a large amount of salt. If the Aquatic Ape hypothesis, which I wrote about in another section of this book, is true, then humans often had access to salt. Maybe it's not much of an issue whether something's salty or not?

R might bring up associations. A few weeks of sitting by the fire in the evening, listening to hits from the 60s and 70s with Bob Marley at the fore, listening to conversations about hitchhiking, or in which country you can make good money working in orchards, or whether there'll finally be a pilgrimage of caravans to India (the word's been going round for years, but no-one's organised it yet) can bore you to death. However, from time to time you might meet wonderful and interesting people, so I'm not too fussed about the seeming boredom of it all. Besides, you can always turn away and go to the woods.

The organisers of R have some kind of sixth sense. Although they usually lead rather laid-back and hedonistic lives, they have a lot of silence, peace, and sensitivity to them, which allows for them to sense the spirit of a place, its *genius loci*. These places are as a rule out of the way and difficult to reach by car, which leads to the formation of a separate caste of those who own big cars, vans, and lorries and live in them, and don't have to bother with another hour of walking to the main camp. Thanks to this sixth sense the spots in which R take place are wild, beautiful and usually located in the presence of both mountain pastures and forest. These places are worthy of a true Indian. It's worse in terms of water. Spots near large rivers tend to be out of the question, because they are less wild and more easily accessible. What remains are mountain waterfalls, small lakes and springs, with the exception of an R organised by the great river San in Tworylne in the Bieszczady Mountains. The other Polish R also took place in a valley, but for instance the Italian and Bulgarian gatherings were organised high up in the mountains. In Italy, they were located in beechwood and berry patches; in Bulgaria, they took place in the spruce treeline, just like in the Tatras! It's interesting to spend the night shivering in places we travel to in the summer for their guaranteed good weather.

The concept of a large tribe in which food is free and there is no violence is a fiction. The gathering takes place in ideal or nearly ideal conditions – in the summer, in a nice place, with no need for self-defence (at least not in Europe – in America there can be trouble with police and forestry). Food is bought from local farmers and shops (which is more than welcomed by the locals) with money brought from the outside, from 'Babylon'. The camp goes on for a month and then packs up. It is, then, a temporary utopia. One of the few that work, because it does not aspire to permanence.

It would be truly utopian to attempt to survive on food available solely from surrounding nature. It's impossible to feed three thousand people on berries and roots from a forest of 250 acres. It would be difficult even to sustain a single small family. Such thoughts often came to mind when spending time in R. The food was, to my taste, disgusting – too much undercooked cabbage, too many half-raw oats. Too little of everything. I supplemented my diet. At the Croatian gathering, I ate leaves: sorrel, thistles, nettles. In Italy, I ate roots of the Alpine avens, inflorescences of silver thistles, orchid bulbs, lizards, blueberries and grasshoppers. In Bulgaria, like in Croatia, I ate grasshoppers and leaves. I guess eating the grasshoppers was against the vegetarian message of R. To me, it seemed innocent and promoted self-sufficiency and ecological eating. I must have looked pretty odd: naked, with red stripes painted on my face, carrying a big paper bag to stop the grasshoppers from jumping out (and made of paper for ecological reasons) in my left hand and an enamel cup in my right, for the berries. When people asked: 'What are you doing, brother', I'd say I was picking fruit. I did bring a whole cup of berries with me, but I also had the bag with about six or seven hundred grasshoppers. In the morning, I'd make a small fire, heat up a saucepan and pour out the grasshoppers. After a few minutes of being tossed over the fire, they would stop jumping and get very hot. Then I'd throw in the berries with some sugar. It was a sweet dish of meat and fruit. Unfortunately I couldn't be bothered with preparing the same for lunch and dinner, so afterwards I'd just eat the cabbage.

In Italy, I began my workshop career. R seemed like the perfect place to pass on my knowledge about wild edible plants – I'd already considered doing it in Croatia. But it was in Italy that I finally plucked up the courage. I had to shout out at three thousand people during lunchtime, while they sat in four concentric circles, repeating my announcement every hundred metres, that is, quite a few times: 'I'm running workshops about eating wild edible plants, meet me after lunch in the main camp'. The time wasn't entirely clear, but oh well, it was 'R time', an hour here or there… So I waited. Soon about a dozen arrived, saying that there are still people coming, then another ten people saying there are more people coming, a third, seventh, tenth group… In the end, 150 people turned up. So I ran my workshops barefoot, leading a half-naked, multilingual group through forests and fields, and shouted out to them in the languages I knew, in Polish, English, Russian, and in Latin, of course. I added 'o' instead of 'um' to Latin names, because that usually immediately translates them into Italian or Spanish, and I knew a few names in French and German. The Polish would shout, 'O, gołąbki', the Russians, 'Vot, sooroyeshki', while the Germans would ask, 'Was ist das?'. When I showed them cattails, some Austrian woman began to worry about the legality of what we were doing, because in Austria cattail is under strict protection. I had to explain to her that it isn't protected in Italy, and after all you know what Italy's like, no-one gives a sh…, with the mafia and all. When we reached a lake and I started talking about water mint, the crowd began to rapidly undress and disperse into the lake. Meanwhile, I picked the mint, put it inside a book, and forgot about it. It survived another week in my damp backpack. I put it in a glass and it took root. It's still growing really well in my garden.

R is a great field for sociological, pan-European observation. It reveals national habits. The Jews made a temple out of a tarpaulin so that people could come and meditate, regardless of their religion. The Germans organised the campsites, commanding people to dig shit-pits. The French drank coffee together, closed up in *un tipi*. The Austrians had an open coffee-shop with free coffee for everyone. The Poles, especially the youths, who are mainly into free food and coffee, were their main clients. In Bulgaria, I met two punks from somewhere in Podhale: 'Mate, we've got it sorted. This guy lives over there. He has a goat. He gives us milk, offers us moonshine, and for now it's for free. We go to this old lady at the bottom of the village. We bought a rooster off her. When this R's over we'll make a sacrificial killing and then chicken soup. She gives us potatoes. Cause you know, we're 'Slav brothers''. It was raining when I arrived at the Italian R, but the brotherhood was there. I was given warm tea at the *welcome centre*, and three Italians took me to a small two-person tent. They dug into their sleeping bags and took out baguettes filled with ham and opened a bottle of wine. 'Want some?', they asked. 'It's R.' One of them said: 'This is Italy, not R. Wine very important. Ham very important. Good for you.'

Still, I always meet people faithful to the R diet. They spend years sustaining themselves on flatbreads, fruit, and cereals. They are vegetarian, vegan, fruitarian, rawist. As a meat lover who doesn't like to think about the death of animals, I admire them but my body won't accept it. I need some meat, or at least dairy, in my diet. I talked to a girl who has been eating apples and carrots for a year. She didn't even look anorexic. These people are more primitive than the primitive (whose diet is 50% meat), and even more

67

primitive than chimpanzees (whose diet contains insects). They're at the gorilla stage.

Bushmen

'Bushmen' is a derogatory, disparaging term, although Westerners have close to no knowledge about these people and we are free from stereotypes about them that would match those of a Plains Indian wearing plumes, a little Pygmy jumping on felled trees in a tropical rainforest, or a naked Australian Aborigine in the desert – about them.

The so-called Bushmen belong to the Khoi-San language family and currently, in order to emphasise and respect the distinctions between different groups, their own names for themselves are most frequently in use. In this chapter, I'll discuss the /Gui, //Gana, Ju/ 'hoansi and the Tyua, people who until recently travelled through the dry regions of south-west Africa, living in small, short-term settlements made of semi-circular huts covered with dry grass. Signs such as '/' and '!' are used in the written names of Khoi-San languages to denote click sounds which are characteristic of this language family.[12]

The /Gui and //Gana live on the territory of Botswana. Laurens van der Post was the first to study them in his 1958 book 'The Lost World of the Kalahari', which was based on a few of his expeditions to these people, a group previously considered extinct.

---

[12] Lee, R.B., Daly, R. (ed.) 1999. *The Cambridge Encyclopaedia of Hunters and Gatherers.* Cambridge: Cambridge University Press.

Until 1979, the time of their settlement, the tribes discussed were basically pure hunter-gatherers. The average group of travellers was made up of about forty people. Their journeys were strongly determined by the infrequent presence of water and wild vegetables, a rarity on the Kalahari 'desert'. Here the term desert is understood in a wide sense, more as a very dry savannah overgrown with grass, the occasional bush, and trees from the *Acacia, Albizia* and *Bauhinia* genera.

Like most Bushmen, these peoples mostly feed on different parts of plants. The most important ones are the bulbs of *Cucumis kalahariensis* and *Coccinia rehmannii*, the nuts of *Bauhinia petersiana* and *Tylosema esculentum*, the fruit of *Grewia flava, G. retinervis* and *Ochna pulchra*, wild melons *Citrullus lanatus* and *Acanthosicyos naudiniana*, and the bulbous plants of the *Ledebouria* genus. They also eat mushrooms, especially desert truffles of the *Terfezia* genus.

Although men spend three to five days a week – between five and twelve hours a day – on hunting, which is similar to the weekly amount of time that women spend gathering wild edible plants, collected for between an hour and five hours every day, the contribution of hunted meat to the overall calorie intake is only 20%. Men hunt around fifty species of animals. Their methods are varied: they use bows and poisoned arrows, hooked sticks, spears, traps, battue or even chase animals and catch them in their bare hands. These species are mainly mammals and birds of different sizes.

Although like among hunter-gatherers, marriages among these peoples are primarily monogamous, polygamy is common and the institution of *zaaku* is particularly interesting here. It consists of commonplace extramarital relationships. At first, they are kept secret. In later phases, they lead to divorce or polygamy or to an institutional exchange of partners and goods between the two 'monogamous' marriages like in the West.

Sadly, since the 70s of the XX century, due to catastrophic droughts, an increase in the tribe's population, settlement programmes, access to drinking water and alcohol, this tribe's way of living has changed for good.

Further to the north-west, on the border of Botswana and Namibia, live the Ju/'hoans. Until recently, they were hunter-gatherers, and are now mainly farmers and shepherds who were lucky enough to have their primitive way of life captured by anthropologists in its final stages. It is on the basis of information about the lives of these people that Sahlins originally formulated his affluent society hypothesis, for their diet, amount of exercise and low rate of illnesses rendered them some of the healthiest people in the world. It is only diseases that were introduced to them later, such as tuberculosis, that decreased their welfare.

Like for previously discussed Bushmen tribes, plants were the Ju/'hoansi's source of food. The fruits of the mongongo tree (*Ricinodendron rautanenii)* were especially precious to them. They would first cook the pulp to make a soup and then roast the seeds it contained, which are apparently very tasty.

The civilizational transformations of the second half of the XX century and the activity of various governments led to their forced settlement, destitution, alcoholism and illnesses. However, some families in the eighties and nineties began to return to territories that had been taken away from them, and with external help, especially from the

Nyae Nyae Development Foundation of Namibia, they began to stop their total disintegration through a combination of gathering, hunting, shepherding, and even ecotourism.

The Tyua tribe lives East of the Ju/'hoansi, on the borders of Botswana and Zimbabwe. They are sometimes called the River Bushmen. These people have upheld economic relations with Bantu farmers for centuries and since 1929 a large part of them have been exiled from their territories through the formation of Zimbabwe Wankie Game Reserve (now Hwange National Park). The Tyua now sustain themselves mainly through farming, shepherding and wage labour, complementing their diet with hunting and gathering. However, hunting was delegalised for them several dozen years ago and has always led to conflict, including arrests. In 1979, the Botswanan government issued special licences which allowed them to hunt, but nevertheless officials and the police still abused their powers over the tribe. Until recently, the Tyua ate 83 species of plants, 52 species of mammals, 18 species of fish, seven species of reptiles, eight species of insects, and three species of fish.

The Tasaday hoax

When writing about hunter-gatherers and their contemporary followers, it's also worth mentioning a case of fake hunter-gatherers – the story of the so-called *Tasaday controversy* concerning a tribe from the Philippines, who had apparently until recently lived like the last cavemen, and which is most likely a hoax.[13]

The Tasaday people were first discovered in 1971 by Manuel Elizalde Junior, the head of PANAMIN, an organisation appointed by president Marcos, the purpose of which was to protect ethnic minorities in the Philippines. He reported on the existence of a group of hunter-gatherers living in the Cotabao forest near Mindanao. This group was made up of 25 people. In the next few months, it became a large point of interest to the world media, and many journalists and anthropologists, always 'taken care of' by Elizalde, had the chance to admire this tribe in its caves. The only person to dispute the discovery was the Filipino anthropologist Zeus Salazar, but he was not admitted access to the tribe. From 1972 until the end of Marcos' dictatorship in 1986, nobody was allowed contact with the tribe and a securely guarded reserve was formed to protect it.

The Swiss anthropologist Oswald Iten, the German journalist Walter Unger and the photographer Jay Ullal were the first to attempt to expose the hoax. The latter two, when they made an expected appearance, found people who were nearly naked, wearing only skirts made of grass. A week later, arriving unannounced, they photographed the same family in normal 'western' clothes.

The Tasaday are indeed a small ethnic group and their way of life does in many respects possess a primitive character. They are primitive farmers – hoe-farmers – who also make use of the forest's resources. But they have been

---

[13] Berreman, G. 1999. The Tasaday controversy. In: R.B. Lee, R Daly (ed.), *The Cambridge Encyclopaedia of Hunters and Gatherers.* Cambridge: Cambridge University Press, pp. 457-464.

used for the purpose of a kind of hoax, presented as primeval cavemen who don't know farming. The Tasaday controversy had an impact on many anthropologists, especially since at first many of them were tricked, and treated the discovery of the Tasaday seriously in their writing. According to Barreman, it was also difficult to completely refute this cynical manipulation throughout the years. It was only the accumulation of a large amount of evidence, linguistic and anthropological inaccuracies, that undermined the famed claims about the Tasaday. The question of whether anthropological research and discoveries are worthy of trust if the Tasadays managed to 'trick' nearly every anthropologist has even been asked in a BBC show. The difficulties with debunking the Tasaday myth were also purely practical: fear of defamation lawsuits or revenge, consisting in, for example, being refused entry to the Philippines. A conference about the Tasaday was held in the Philippines, and a special volume devoted to them, in which the alleged scam was treated rather lightly, was published by the American Anthropological Association. The volume's editor, T. N. Headland, emphasized that the Tasadays themselves weren't deceiving the anthropologists on purpose.

Banana and calamus

Among thousands of plant species that are similar to each other, there are some characteristic ones that are difficult to mistake, and at the same time incredibly useful. The banana, for example. The banana tree is a large plant that can reach over a dozen metres in height, but it's a gigantic perennial rather than a tree.

It is generally known as a plant with edible fruits. Its flowers are also edible and are sold as a vegetable in Thai markets. Its leaves can be used in many ways, as natural plates for meals (India), for rolling up dishes that are roasted on hot coals, or even as short-term hut coverings. The banana seems to be hard to replace. Its floury fruits with a unique taste and massive, non-poisonous leaves make it a plant of great value. In our climate, we could use other large leaves instead of banana leaves, but when we look around us, there aren't all that many plants with big leaves to choose from. Horseradish works really well. It's actually traditionally used in Poland for baking bread on and its leaves are wrapped round fish grilled in fire. My daughter Nasim loves to eat grilled sausages and hold them in horseradish leaves.

What other leaves were used in Poland for baking bread on? As research by the Polish Ethnographical Atlas has shown, in addition to horseradish, cabbage was widely used, along with the fragrant leaves of calamus in the north-east. Much less often, maple, sycamore, and oak leaves were used in some villages. I've also heard of the use of grape vines for this, which is probably a more recent fashion, but may well be a traditional practice in the South, as after all both the Balkans and the Middle East are famous for their stuffed grape leaves – *sarma* or *dolma*. Just like we use cabbage for our Polish *gołąbki*, the Southerners use grape vines, the Romanians and the Hutsuls sometimes stuff the bitter leaves of coltsfoot, while in Moldova they even used to use marigolds for this purpose. An impressive few dozen species of leaves are used to wrap sarma on the edge of Europe and Turkey![14]

Why, when writing about naturalness, am I writing about stuffed leaf dishes? Because the leaf as an architectonic product or a substitute for paper or vessel is something natural, deeply primitive. Before bread was made, rice was cooked or stuffing it in leaves was invented, meat, fish, insects and bulbs were roasted on embers.

Besides roasting on the surface of the ground, the practice of pit cooking is also widespread among primitive people even of places very far away from each other. The Maori, Australian Aborigines, and Indians from the coast of the Pacific all did this.

They would make a pit, often surrounded by stones, in which they would light a fire and then remove at least some of the hot embers. They would make a layer of green leaves with bulbs or meat between them. Meals cooked in such a way have an amazing aroma and usually cook evenly (it's easy to burn a lot of things when roasting them over a fire). Another strength (and at once weakness) of this method is the long prep time. We put the produce in in the evening, and breakfast is ready for us in the morning. Burying food in the ground is also a primitive method of its preservation. In Poland, too, cabbage used to be pickled directly in pits, similarly to how the people of Siberia prepared wild plants. There were also cases of meat being conserved by burying a

[14] Sõukand, R., Pieroni, A., Biró, M., Dénes, A., Dogan, Y., Hajdari, A., Kalle, R., Reade, B., Mustafa, B., Nedelcheva, A. and Quave, C.L., 2015. An ethnobotanical perspective on traditional fermented plant foods and beverages in Eastern Europe. *Journal of Ethnopharmacology*, 170: 284-296.

whole animal underground. Peat is especially useful for this purpose. Mammoths conserved in peat, which are probably still good to eat, have been found many times in Siberia. A good stomach can take a lot... Once, during a botany class, I stole a piece of coconut from a friend. I was surprised that the meat was so hard (although it did taste of coconut). Only then did I notice a stamp on the shell – Carskiy Imperatorsky Universeetet. It was a museum specimen.

Hunter-gatherers for cash

It's not always through farming that wild hunter-gatherers end up abandoning elements of their primitive way of life. In many contemporary cases, they jump straight into sales, which is probably the easier route. Rather than being a nomadic hunter, they become a nomad in search of employment in 'Babylon'. This often happens to, for instance, the sea nomads of Indochina. There's also an intermediary option to hunt and gather for cash, maintaining one's lifestyle but gaining new goods, such as shotguns, beads, firewater, rice, sugar, or flour. That's the way both Native Americans and indigenous peoples of Siberia traded with Europeans. Hunter-gatherer societies from Borneo have been supplying goods to traders for the last few hundred years. The nomadic Raji of Nepal have specialised – they collect wild honey and exchange some of it for rice while supplementing their diet with wild game. Societies could only trade when not isolated from farmers, which wasn't possible in Australia (they would have probably had to make trips to New Guinea). An ancient group of ancient hunter-gatherers related to the Nepalese Raji, the Raute, trade wooden bowls carved from stumps of woodland trees. They take them to villages and exchange for the amount of rice they can fit in a bowl. As for meat, they hunt for monkeys – macaques and langurs. They don't show strangers how they hunt or eat monkey meat. This is a way of protecting themselves from being observed in situations that their farmer neighbours, who don't eat monkey meat, might find disgusting.[15] Living in the modern world on the border of farmyard territory, it's best to eat what they don't so as to not get in their way. Find a niche – mice, rats, monkeys, or – like the European Roma – hedgehogs. I think that in modern Europe, while a hedgehog-devourer would sooner or later be chased by some environmental organisation, a rat-eater would enjoy great popularity. Sadly, we lack such people and it's easier to survive in big cities by eating good quality food from dustbins which rats feed on than by eating the rats themselves.

The departure from a hunter-gatherer lifestyle can be seasonal. Pygmies spend part of the year working on plantations, and the other part hunting in the forest.

In terms of their diet, these partly wild groups hardly differ from Polish professional poachers and the inhabitants of closed-down State farms in the Recovered Territories that were widely discussed in the media, in which after the fall of Communism, people lived solely off wild berries and mushrooms... and probably poaching. The writer of these words could perhaps also qualify as a 'gatherer for cash'. A large part of my income comes from the sale of the seeds of

---

[15] Reinhard, J. 1974. The Raute: Notes on a Nomadic Hunting and Gathering Tribe of Nepal. *Journal of Himalayan Studies,* 2(4): 233-271.

wild plants that neither I nor my clients eat, but rather sow in their gardens to have beautiful field and meadow flowers. It's true that some of these have been gathered for food, but it would be an expensive diet. I can gather half a kilogram or a kilogram of most species in a day. That's like a day's work for a kilogram of wholemeal flour. I don't think it's worth abandoning civilization for something like that. Which of the flower seeds that I collect are fit to eat? Some are poisonous. The edible ones include various species of vetch which, after a lot of soaking and cooking, can be made into what tastes like bean soup, poppy and evening primrose which work well in sandwiches, common bistort and sorrel for groats.

Making cash out of some of one's game and gatherings is a good, 'modern' survival strategy. It allows for a life on the go and for the preservation of a culture associated with hunting and gathering. One could become part of a caste, tolerated or even prized. Hunter-gatherers sometimes come up with new ways of making use of their environments. For instance, the Moken People of the Surin Islands from between Thailand and Burma started to dive and collect large shells to sell them to tourists but they have now been forbidden to do so.

Paleo diet

Over ten years ago, when my fascination with the hunter-gatherers began, I supplemented my diet with wild roots, leaves, and run-over frogs and hedgehogs, because I wanted to become independent from the system, from money and the whole chain of human responsibilities. It was only many years later that I began to appreciate the health benefits of the primitive human diet and the dangers of straying too far from it.

When I started out, I believed that one day, once I fully 'master' the art of foraging for wild plants, I will finally become self-sufficient. I had just started a family, had my first daughter, and didn't have much time or energy for digging and washing small roots for six hours a day. Most of my calories came from pasta, bread, and potatoes, around which I created different dishes assembled from easily accessible wild leaves. In November 2004, when I attended the funeral of one of my greatest masters, my past supervisor, professor Faliński, thanks to a meetup with my old friend from back when I lived at the Professor's research station, I was introduced to Marek Konarzewski, who divided his work between Białowieża and Białystok. Professor Konarzewski then gave me access to his soon-to-be-published book, *Na początku był głód* [*At first there was a famine*], a great evolutionary story of the history of the human diet and the effects of departure from it (for example, of eating bread).

His book is very anti-vegetarian. It contains many arguments for the importance of meat in our diet (healthy meat, of course, not the factory products we buy in shops). I was then very pro-vegetarian (although I had never been vegetarian). Under the influence of a few hours of conversation with professor Konarzewski, I became a freshly converted meat-eater (I guess I'd always liked meat, but it seemed to be an unnecessary, costly form of sponsorship of the death of animals).

The arguments were simple – I was becoming increasingly overweight with high odds of developing hereditary diabetes. A primitive diet apparently solves both of these problems. Until then, I'd been only partly on the right path. Wild vegetables, yes. But bread and pasta need to be replaced with wild game... If we accept killing animals at least to some extent and agree that a return to a primitive human diet means a return to consuming meat enriched with fruit and vegetables, without the spoilt products of civilization such as bread, alcohol, and sweets, a return to such a diet should be tempting. It already has a name – it's usually called the Paleolithic diet – and many followers. Lorain Cordain, the author of *The Paleo Diet*[16], is its most famous propagator.

Comparative studies of diets of different groups of hunter-gatherers show that they sourced over half of their calories from meat. Meat contributed to less – about a third of caloric content – only in a few tropical and subtropical groups. But this isn't the kind of meat we usually buy in the shop: sausage, bacon or chicken. These are bodies of wild animals. This kind of meat is leaner than 'shop-bought' meat. It contains a lot more protein. If we want to eat meat more like wild meat, the simplest thing to do is buy a deer. But of course that's expensive. Another solution is eating products such as chicken breasts or liver or other offal which contain negligible amounts of fat. But here we might fall into a trap. Although they contain barely any fat, they are nevertheless usually products of the factory farming of animals, which are fed on antibiotics and synthetic mixes. The same goes for fish such as trout, carp, or tilapia, which

---

[16] A list of this author's books and articles can be found at www.thepaleodiet.com.

are bred on special food in cramped spaces. As a result of our oceans increasingly being used as dustbins, even fish in the open sea are not free from contamination. It's also dangerous to eat too much liver. A lot of environmental poisons accumulate in this organ, especially if the animal has had a long life – so this goes not for young chicken, but especially horse meat (as horses are usually slaughtered at an old age).

Don't think that choosing an 'eco-chicken', an *organic* or *bio* product, will be of any help either! Even ecological chickens are usually fed mostly grain, at least in the winter. Omega-6 fatty acids contained in grains can contribute to cardiovascular diseases and outweigh the beneficial omega-3. The meat and eggs of animals that are fed grains isn't wild, even if they lived in the fresh air, ran around freely and led happy lives. A wild chicken is a chicken we might find in the jungle of Indochina – jumping around in trees and gobbling up worms. If you want to own a bird like that yourself, move to the edge of the forest, make a large chicken coop and let the chickens into it in the springtime. By autumn, you will have great meat, enough to make a few saucepans of broth. Too bad that foxes are everywhere nowadays – the breeding of 'forest' chickens is a dying practice in my village... You can tell from the taste of the eggs.

Wild poultry can also be found on the side of the road in the form of dead pheasants. In England, where there are more pheasants, many people have started to collect these dead birds, but it's harder to rely on them here in Poland. I've only got hold of such a rarity a few times. Of course pheasants also steal grain from farmers, which was proved to me by the sight of what I found in the aviary of such a slaughtered pheasant. However, a large part of their diet is made up of invertebrates and wild plants. After two hours of cooking pheasant broth I only spotted one drop of fat – now that's what I call a wild bird!

I ate my first roadkill pheasant in England. My house in Norwich was really cold and we supplemented the central heating with a fireplace. I gathered wood for it in the form of firewood from a park in the city and from Thetford Forest. I found the pheasant on my way to Thetford Forest, but my friend took it, as I'd been reading too much on botulism – the effects of infection with toxins produced by *Clostridium botulinum* bacteria. These can sometimes be found in old meat and old vegetable preserves and cause a rather unpleasant death. I waited for three days. Our friend was still alive. The pheasant was big, she got bored of it and gave me the leftovers of her goulash. Since finding out that wild game is so hard that pheasant should be kept in the cellar for two weeks to make it easier to eat, I have been more keen on roadkill.

Hedgehogs are also tempting to eat. They have delicious brown meat (hence the word *hedgehog* – hog of the hedges). However, I'm a little afraid of rabies. You never know if it's been run over as a result of rabid craze. The first time I gutted a hedgehog, I did it in thick rubber gloves. It gave me 300g of tasty goulash. The second time, I grilled it whole. The spikes stank a little, but there was some meat there. Gypsies prepare hedgehogs in clay. But we still need to consider whether hedgehogs and pheasants don't contain too much lead. There's always something wrong... And then there's rabies, although this isn't a problem in the UK. Rabid animals are probably and easier victim for cars. I heard that it is very difficult to get infected by rabies just by cutting the meat of an animal, but who knows. In the last 10 years since writing the Polish version of this book, my knowledge of roadkill has grown immensely... I've eaten a cat, a squirrel, and various other yummy creatures. Their meat is always delicious and devoid of the bad karma and greed of the meat industry.

Grasshoppers are probably the cleanest meat in Poland, if caught in the hills far from the main road. They feed on wild mountain grass and smell wonderful after roasting – like sprats, only cleaner, as sprats live in the polluted ocean. Grasshoppers are just really hard to catch. Even catching 200 per hour cannot cover our energy expenditure. If my calculations are right, we would have to spend over 24h a day catching them, unless we perfect our hunting methods. Grasshoppers enjoyed great popularity with some Native American tribes of the West of the USA. In the state of Utah, the wind would blow them from the plains into salt lakes in which they would drown and could be collected by the bucket.

Hadza

The Hadza people, a tribe of around a thousand members, live in the hills of northern Tanzania. They are tall, slim, dark-skinned hunter-gatherers who came to the attention of Westerners only at the beginning of the XX century. Until the 60s, they lived exclusively from hunting and gathering. Now, they supplement their diets by cultivating fields of corn and sweet potato... They do still hunt when possible, but they have commercial poachers to compete with. The latter have already managed to eliminate the rhinoceros and most elephants.

The Hadza live in a country that conforms to stereotypes of the beginnings of humanity. They live in the dry African savannah, in hills filled with game. Their arrows kill impala, zebras, buffalos, elands and zebus. They don't limit themselves to killing. They will happily eat carrion, for instance by stealing it from lions. The Hadza don't use guns or traps. They are seasoned 'race-walkers'. They are able to wear out ungulates with constant pursuit. Antelopes are good sprinters but they cannot bear the overheating it causes. In the meantime, women collect shoots of rhizomes and fruit, especially baobab fruit. The Hadza are connoisseurs of mammal meat. In contrast to many other African tribes, they barely eat insects, reptiles, fish, or freshwater molluscs.[17]

The Hadza currently live partly in permanent settlements under the pressure of the government and are partly still on the go. In the 60s, they all travelled in small groups of just over a dozen members. They would move camp every two or three weeks. The Hadza hold the accumulation of material possessions in particular contempt and share all of their food and goods. They also gamble, playing a game called *lukucuko*, in which the bet is placed on arrows, knives, or pipes. Gambling seems to have accompanied humans from the very beginning, and different games in which weapons, symbolic objects or food are used as stakes can be found in many primitive cultures.

---

[17] Lee, R.B., Daly, R. (ed.) 1999. *The Cambridge Encyclopaedia of Hunters and Gatherers.* Cambridge: Cambridge University Press.

Among the Thompson Indians, who live in the mountains of north-west North America, women gambled with trout lily (*Erythronium*) bulbs they would dig out themselves. As a result, some women would return with double the amount of food, others with nothing.

The Hadza are an ultraegalitarian society whose individual members live on equal terms, regardless of their age or sex. A kind of communist ideal. The Hadza divide only rituals, like many other tribes. Men and women have separate, secret rituals such as female genital mutilation. A ceremony that brings the sexes together is called the *epeme* dance and is conducted in darkness. Anthropologists are fascinated by them mainly because of their faithfulness to hunting in an environment which greatly resembles the beginnings of human life, and of course because of their carrion-eating.

Nudity

As my conversations with different people have shown, nudity is one of the things most associated with wildness. The theme of shame and concealing nudity also appears in the Book of Genesis. But is it really that important? What's the issue here?

The human was, at first, naked, and human evolution began with the evolution of the nude human. In some warmer parts of the world there are still cultures 'more' naked than the European, in which people are not ashamed of leaving their breasts and genitalia uncovered.

Nudity is an exciting topic for the European, because the more dressed are at first always excited by the less dressed. Just like the sight of hair, knees, thighs, or shoulders of Europeans for guests from more conservative Muslim countries. This also reminds me of the excitement I feel when I see women's legs in the city streets during the first warm days of spring after they have been covered up during the winter.

Exposing nearly everything doesn't count as total nakedness. In some cultures, the removal of a loincloth or some head garment decides whether a person counts as naked.

The first argument used against nudity by its enemies is the existence of a sort of natural shame, but we can disprove this through observing the behaviour of people in 'naked' cultures.

The second argument is to do with 'protection of privacy', a little like the protection of personal information. 'Why should anyone look at my small/large penis' – some say. Again, it's relative. A proponent of the niqab (the Muslim veil) can ask: 'Why should anyone look at my wife's face?' Maybe there's a happy medium somewhere? Maybe our civilization has found it in a kind of partial tolerance. The happy middle is more likely to lie somewhere in the middle, rather than far to the side, especially not the Saudi side.

The real reasons for covering the body are much more concrete. People from cold countries began to wear clothes as soon as they learned to remove the skin from animals and make it into clothing. It is not possible to conquer Siberia in the nude. The cultures of the far north and of all countries with frosty winter, that is, for instance, at least two thirds of Europe, have lost touch with total nudity since their very beginnings, with the exception of the Finnish, Estonians, and Russians, who cultivate the sauna. As humans have inhabited cold Europe for the past few dozen thousand years and have been eating bread only for a little more than ten thousand years, the coat may be more integral to our mentality than farming. A naked human in the frost risks death. A naked human in a low temperature above zero, for example 5 or 12 degrees Celsius, is at risk of using up a great deal of their energy even if they are used to this temperature, so they need to eat more than those who are dressed.

What about occasional nudity? Well, if one goes around in clothes all the time, this at first natural nudity becomes more exciting, a special moment guarded with a kind of taboo. There are, however, large cultural differences in approach to nudity in cold countries. In aforementioned Finland, Estonia, Russia, Japan and Korea, countries where steam rooms are popular and people pass their winters by in the sauna and for millennia now, having warmed up, caper about in the snow, nudity is not shocking but is merely a temporary state, a time for play and hygiene. Meanwhile cold countries such as Poland and England, to which the sauna is a foreign invention, have a culture that has ingrained a whole range of inhibitions in their inhabitants, which are only beginning to be broken down nowadays.

Covering up is also a way of protection from sexual aggression. Each layer of clothing gives both the offender and the victim extra time.

There is another rarely mentioned reason for wearing clothes: parasites. Sitting naked, it's easier to spread the eggs of parasites on an improperly washed bum than if we're sitting in clothes.

People are trying to change the extent of the taboo that surrounds nudity. I myself am a great enemy of it, because other than practical inconveniences in cold climates, nudity makes sense in hot climates. The body breathes well and it's easier to keep it clean. Besides, a lot of people have an inescapable need to look at naked bodies. And this is not only to do with sexual fascination. It's the need to see people in full view, not divided up by their underwear. It's really refreshing. It's like saying we shouldn't be allowed to look at flowers. It doesn't seem to cause too many practical issues, but it would be a shame nevertheless...

Of course northern foreigners need clothes in the tropics to not burn to a crisp. Constant contact with sunlight seriously increases our chances of getting skin cancer.

An individual's attempt at shifting the nudity taboo may be penalised in some countries, or end in aggression from other people – but not always.

My slightly insane friend approached my sister a few years ago asking whether she could film his baptism for a mountain hermit. Sensing that something was going to happen, she took me with her. Everything was going to take place on the town square in Krosno. It was February, with temperatures around zero. The friend arrived pretty exposed – only his hips were covered with a fir wreath. He held a birch stick in his hand and confessed that he had smeared himself with sheep dung instead of clothes. He was hoping to provoke the Philistines and for an action to be brought out against him by the local authorities. He danced and lay on the ground. People paid no attention to him and neither did the local authorities. One small girl asked her mum: 'Why is that man so strangely dressed?' – 'What man?' –

the mother asked – 'I can't see any man'. My friend got very cold and despite his fascination with naturalness and nudity and his great desire to move the masses, he was forced to get dressed.

I assume that on nudist beaches, those on which nakedness is required, there are few issues with how to behave. An unwanted erection might be a problem for some men, but that's only a compliment to the women, and besides, this rarely happens once they become used to their environments.

Issues to do with behaviour or so-called savoir-vivre arise in mixed situations. Take for example the R gatherings, which I write about in another section of this book. These gatherings are organised under the admirable slogans of love and freedom. There's not much aggression in them and freedom abounds in choice of dress, which is manifested by the presence of a large amount of naked bodies. Naked people can be seen wandering around the campsite, eating naked in a circle, and serving food. Groups of naked people stand naked in line for the shower – a hose pipe with water running from some spring above. A great deal of gradation can be seen in the attitudes of different people and nations. Some wash alone in some out-of-the-way stream, always dressed. Others undress only in this large public shower but nowhere else. Then there are those who walk around the campsite naked but get dressed for mealtimes in the circle (I'm not sure why but this is the group I belonged to, probably because I was in search of the 'golden mean'). Finally, there are those who come to eat naked but serve food clothed. And of course those who are always nude. The Germans are overrepresented on the naked side, while the Polish and English are most often amongst those always clothed. But that's just a statistically unimportant observation...

It's interesting that men with long penises and flat-chested women dominate the group of those who attend R naked. There are surprisingly few men with small penises, perhaps because they are ashamed. And why are there so few women with large breasts? Maybe they feel people's gaze more intensely? Maybe it's uncomfortable and tiring for them? Or maybe the flat-chested ones are trying to validate themselves through nudity? Women with a more masculine appearance and small breasts probably also have more testosterone, which may make them more determined to reach difficult-to-access mountainous areas, where these hippie gatherings take place. So maybe the large-breasted women don't come to R at all? I have only seen a few each time. Besides, when naked, these differences level out – large breasts, small breasts, etc. Healthy and young bodies are simply beautiful. People, you're all beautiful!

Natural family

What does a primitive family living in accord with nature look like? Gorillas have harems in which a strong male guards his females. Orangutans live in pairs. Chimpanzees get with everyone, regardless of their sex. What about people? We're genetically closer to chimps, so we might expect similar sexual chaos. Something of the kind was suggested by first theoreticians of the history of the family and of marriage, for instance the American anthropologist Lewis Henry Morgan.

Meanwhile, anthropologists studying hunter-gatherers often find 'normal' relationships between men and women. Monogamy (the 'one wife – one husband' model) is widespread. The difference between monogamous primitive tribes and modern Western society lies in the fact that we treat polygamy as illegal, while it is commonplace for the vast majority of primitive tribes, although most men have only one wife. So the primitive model is roughly the same as the Muslim one: Islam allows for four wives, but it rarely happens in practice. After all, there is a similar amount of women and men. Polygamy became more frequent in farming societies. Some men simply got richer than others, owned more land, and the offspring of multiple wives was able to cultivate it. Hunter-gatherer societies are more egalitarian, hence the predominance of monogamy. There are also advocates of the naturalness of women's promiscuity, such as Christopher Ryan and Cacilda Jethá, the authors of the amazing book *Sex at Dawn: The Prehistoric Origins of Modern Sexuality* (2010), which I highly recommend you read.

However, one must admit that the hunter-gatherers' rites of marriage are less developed than among farmers. They make gifts, move property around, or require temporary service at the in-laws'. Divorces are also frequent. The Aché tribe, in which one woman can have over a dozen husbands in her lifetime, are masters of it.

Does this not resemble our present times of serial monogamy? Maybe contrary to the complaints of older generations, this is how it ought to be. Of course the difference is that current divorces often lead to parents moving to distant cities or countries, while in primitive tribes children remained in the same circle of extended family, and their parents remained in the same or associated group.

The cyclist

They call him the cyclist. He lives in a small town in the south of Poland, where he built a wooden tipi and a wooden shed like a tool shed on his private land. He has no heating. He's been living in an unheated shed, thin as a stick, healthy as a horse, for many years. He once told me that bread and butter are his main source of food. He also drinks herbal tea, depending on the season. He even drinks tea from willow bark when he's ill. He needs money for his gas bottle and for bicycle parts which he has used to cycle across half of Eurasia. If primitive people were very minimal, the cyclist definitely has something in common with them. If there are two anthropologists for each Bushman, he certainly deserves a couple to take care of him, too.

Aché

We love to be on the move. We only sleep once in a place, but if it rains we might sleep several times before moving on. When the rain stops, we hit the undergrowth with our unstrung bows to shake down the waterdrops and frighten the jaguars. We are on the move again.

Bepurangi, member of Aché tribe, 1978[18]

The Aché are one of the last hunter-gatherer tribes of South America. They live in the forests of Eastern Paraguay. These hidden forest people used to be considered cannibals.[19] Little was known about them until the XX century, when they became one of the main subjects of anthropological studies of hunter-gatherers.

Most of the territories they inhabit are subtropical forests with an average temperature of 35° C in summer and 10° C in the coldest months. Even frost can occur a few times a year.

The Aché live in small groups that usually include 7-9 men. Until recently they ate mainly mammal meat. Meat contributes to 78% of calories in their diet. They eat chiefly armadillos, Capuchin monkeys, peccaries, pacas, coatis, and deer. Their other main product is honey, which contributes to 8%. These two foods are sourced only by men, while women are responsible chiefly for sourcing the hearts of palms, palm starch, beetle larvae from the inner cores of palms, and fruit. It's astounding how little of their diet consists in fruit, especially considering that forests are abundant in them – even wild oranges are commonplace there!

As this tribe has been so well quantified, I'll give you some more numbers related to their lives. Men spend

[18] Hill, K. & Hurtado, A.M. 1999. The Aché of Paraguay. In: R.B. Lee, R Daly (ed.), *The Cambridge Encyclopaedia of Hunters and Gatherers.* Cambridge: Cambridge University Press.

[19] Hill, K. & Hurtado, A.M. 1999. The Aché of Paraguay. *op. cit.*

around seven hours a day on work (mostly hunting). Women collect food only for around two hours a day, but they spend another two hours moving camp, and the rest of the time on taking care of children. Aché move camp every day, unless it's very rainy. According to elders, in the past they used to remain in the same spot for a few days more often.

This wandering and constant change has an impact on their personal life. Marriages aren't particularly long-lasting. Until recently, the average woman had twelve husbands in a lifetime! According to anthropologists who studied this tribe, barely any marriage lasted for the whole life of the couple, and the average woman bears children for two to five husbands.

In recent years, the life of the Aché has undergone major changes: their language is being replaced by Guarani, a language widely used in Paraguay. As noted by Hill and Hurtado, elders have decided to maintain only some of their rituals, such as the existence of a kind of godfather, the dominance of meat and honey in their diet, strong identification with their consumption of insect larvae (in contrast to more 'civilised' tribes) and the strong cultural significance of the sharing of food. Catholic and protestant missionaries are also active in Aché reserves, which of course will further hasten the disappearance of its culture.

Burning Man

I've never been to Burning Man, at least not yet. It's a massive festival that takes place in a desert in western USA. Thousands of people, especially artists, go there to create then burn their works and a large figure of a human being at the end of the festival, hence the name Burning Man.

The festival is located in a kind of sterile place. It's inhospitable because of constant heat and lack of water and welcoming because of constant sunshine. The dry heat allows for relaxed clothing or its lack, there's no need for umbrellas, and water can easily be brought along from outside. A similar festival in the East of the States could not be equally successful due to frequent rainfall.

Burning Man is a commercial party and is more organised than Rainbow meetings. However, both here and there, people's ability to self-organise is delightful. Both of these parties are an example of creative chaos.

Burning Man is psychedelia brought to life. It's nearly a social movement of the internet-art-new-age-tribalist kind. The constructions created there tower over even the wildest imagery experienced on LSD, and the ways in which some people paint their bodies belong to the height of achievements of body art in the world. There are so many ways to paint a penis! Or even to hide it, if it's small and easy to conceal in a meadow painted on the thighs. There are so many ways of draping fabrics, hanging beads and stripes off the body, of course in a way that isn't practical in daily life. And there are so many ways of turning women's breasts into spirals, concentric circles, butterflies, flowers, mandalas, and sea anemones.

Modern life spent constantly wrapped up in clothes and on the run somewhere creates a longing for primitive rituals of body modification and body painting. This need seems to be fairly widespread. It is partly satisfied by female makeup and rises to the surface more rarely for men, for example during football matches, when fans paint national flags on their faces.

During my forest workshops we often paint our bodies. The extreme change in appearance gives rise to a natural equivalent of Gurdjieff's 'stop' exercise, when suddenly through the abnormality of our environment we become more aware, rooted in the here and now.

There are many different patterns for body painting. In fact, body painting, in its function and diversity, resembles clothing. Amongst the patterns I've seen I am particularly fascinated by those which run from the armpits along the side of the body along the torso, thighs, and legs, all the way down to the feet. Clothing, with its skirts, stripes, t-shirts and trousers, emphasises the division of the body into an upper part, a middle – taboo – part, and a lower part – the feet. Meanwhile, what fascinates me about the body is the unity of its function, which is emphasised precisely by this kind of oblong pattern, for example a group of lines or a row of dots. We then look more like water creatures, fish, lizards, newts. Another pattern that makes a big impression on me and which I use myself is a bright, white or yellow line along the nose.

Lila

Lila has straw-coloured hair and a long plait. She ran away from the city into the peripheries of Poland. She built a small hut all on her own on a hill by the forest. Not the kind of hut you'd see in the portfolio of an architectural practice, not a log cabin of the kind you see in the average open-air museum, and neither is it a gingerbread house on chicken legs like Baba Yaga's hut. Here is how Lili's cottage was built: first she tied poles together as if to form a tipi. She covered the top with reeds cut down from a roadside ditch. Once the roof was ready, she made the walls beneath it on a circular ground plan. She drove some stakes vertically into the ground, wound some wicker around them and covered them with clay. They had to be quite thick – about half a metre wide. So it looks as if the small fairy-tale cottage under a thatch roof was drawn into a tipi, because their lower ends stick out of the hut. However, we don't usually notice this, seeing only a hut with hand-modelled walls and heart-shaped window. You need to bend over to walk in through the small door, oval at the top. In the centre of the house, the earthen floor is made of stone and the sides are made of clay. There's a fireplace and baskets full of provisions – grains and beans. This is what the life of a Slavic witch looks like.

Why did she run away from the world all the way to its edge? Why did a girl from the city decide to move to the forest for a few years? I don't know. She probably felt she needed to do it, at least for a while. I was captivated by what she does. I'm always delighted when people don't spend their time talking, telling stories, promising, making grand plans, but simply keep going forward.

When I saw her cabin for the first time, I thought: 'She lives in a shelter in the wilderness but buys her lentils in the shop'. Two years later she had a partner, a shelter with goats, and a very big garden to cultivate. From the civilised world, she only kept her phone, charging it every few days in the village shop. For the first few years she used to get away in the winter. She would appear with the first flowers and escape along with the coming of the first frost.

A nomadism between forest and flat. Quite a good invention.

Then they finally spent the winter in the cabin. Under thick duvets, as she later told me. Heat escaped somewhere under the straw roof and cold came off the clay. They installed a stove with a pipe instead of using an open fire. Civilization comes in with small steps, pours in like water through the smallest cracks. 'How come it's so dry inside?' I ask her. She replies: 'First it was damp, but I got fed up and dug tar paper under the walls.'

Tierra del Fuego

The Tierra del Fuego, the southernmost end of South America, is wind-lashed, cold, damp, and oceanic. As recently as the XIX century, it was home to Yamana, one of the most primitive tribes on Earth, and its name comes from the fires that its inhabitants would light to keep warm.

These people have been captured in the diaries of Charles Darwin. His description of a naked woman breastfeeding children with snow falling onto her shoulders is especially famous. The temperature here usually reaches a few degrees Celsius, although frost and snow can appear throughout the year. Rocky fjords are covered with southern beeches (*Nothofagus* spp.). However, it is the sea, not the forest, that is the source of most of their food. Before the arrival of colonisers who killed off most of their resources, around a thousand indigenous inhabitants from this tribe lived here. They hunted a great variety of marine fauna from their canoes: right wales, seals, sea otters, fish, great cormorants and other sea birds, and collected mussels from rocks by the sea. Nevertheless, seals were their main source of sustenance.

The Yamana moved nearly every day. Sometimes they spent whole days on their canoes. Women had an active role in sourcing animal products: they caught fish, mussels, and even birds for food. Women were often, to an equal extent as men, shamans. The tribe lacked a clear chief structure. Families travelled alone or in small groups. Shelters were simple and temporary. Multiple groups would travel through the same territories, so good camping spots, for example those already containing old shelter structures, were reused by the following group.

Because of the incessant search for food and constant travel, larger groups seldom gathered together. They would do so, for example, on the occasion of a large whale being washed ashore.

The first half of the twentieth century, however, caused major changes to the Yamana way of life. Because of the influx of White inhabitants, they became farm workers, mixed with them through marriage, and their language slowly died out. Today, all that remains of their culture are a few people who know the Yamana language and travellers' descriptions of the tribe.

Cat-lover

Whether I go to heaven or hell, I'll definitely meet him there. I was threatened with him from the age of three. A jittery drunk with a silver beard always walking his bike. I was told that he ate children, only naughty ones of course. The box on the back of his bike could probably fit in a three year old. Sometimes he stood in front of the church and begged.

He didn't really eat children. He ate cats. Only now, his culinary preferences make me feel close to him. He was a suburban, self-sufficient hunter. Now I am grey-haired like him. May he rest in peace.

Cannibalism and the placenta

I was always fascinated with cannibals. That's why I ate the placenta after the birth of one of my daughters. It wasn't actually cannibalism but an innocent way of tasting human 'flesh'. Cannibalism isn't good for anything, unless of course one is really hungry or has some magical urge. But it's wild, wild, wild, so it's in keeping with the subject of this book.

I guess it's all Sarah's fault. Both of my daughters were born in England. When Nasim, my first, was born, Sarah said: 'You know, people in England eat placentas, at least those in alternative circles do'. And true enough, the nurse in the hospital in Taunton, accustomed to hippies from Glastonbury, asked:

'Would you like it packed?'

'Yes, please', I replied.

Most of those who say *yes* bury it under a tree, just like primitive tribes did. I have looked for any mention of eating them many times. I always found only about animals, even the herbivores, and the Chinese. I also I found out that among Polish peasants, elder siblings ate them to prevent jealousy. But I can't remember where I read this... Maybe I dreamt it? But I can picture it well enough. A wooden cottage with six children in it, devouring a chunk of meat for the first time in the year.

The human placenta looks a bit like a liver. It tastes like something between a tenderloin and a liver. The one left after Nasim's birth weighted eighty decagrams. I ate a third raw. I ate the second portion like steak tartare, with pepper and egg, except I didn't have the right kind of cucumbers because I was in England. I made a *tikka masala* out of the third, wanting to give it to Sarah. I brought it to hospital but she didn't want it, excusing herself with her vegetarianism, so I ate it.

When we had our second child, she ate half with chilli and ginger, then dried the rest like the Chinese. I laid out a sheet to collect the blood. It gathered up. When Daisy was born, I made a toast of a full glass collected from this sheet.

Walden

By the river Walden in New England, USA, near Concord, there once lived a man called Henry David Thoreau (1817-1862). Some student once lent me his most famous book, *Walden, or Life in the Woods* and that's how my journey with him began. Students often bring interesting things with them. The more you listen– and the more often you get the chance to drink with them – the more you learn and so become a better teacher yourself.

He was an eccentric. He didn't start a family, didn't eat meat, he hated violence, he created the concept of civil disobedience. He loved nature. In search of a return to it (already in the XIX century) and in search of independence, he built a small hut near Walden, with dimensions around 3 x 4 m. Alone. His book is the story of this building process. Thoreau writes about how every architecture student should build a house as part of their course assessment. A century and a half have gone by and his idea still hasn't come to fruition. Thoreau cultivated the land and took his food from it. There is so much love in his prose. Love for people and love for the world. He was one of the few people who loved Native Americans and although his life was so short everyone who runs into the wilderness should think about him for at least a moment. Even though, as local legends holds, he busied himself with building and nutritional self-sufficiency, he was taken care of by his mother who lived nearby and often brought him food or maybe even did his washing for him.

Walden inspired many activists, philosophers, and thinkers. Although Thoreau's experiment with building a house wasn't a long-term success, I will always remember his in-depth thoughts encouraging for students to build their own houses instead of paying rent.

Urban menagerie

I used to live on the tenth floor of a block of flats in Warsaw, a city of two million inhabitants, on Smyczkowa Street. One day my mood was ruined by a foul smell. I quickly identified its source. The rotting body of a pigeon was stuck in the ventilation system. The pigeon is a symbol of nature in the big city, and a symbol of perfect adaptation to it. It used to be a bird of mountainous places. The city is like the mountains – it is natural and contains countless new natural habitats. The pigeon provides a great opportunity for the urban survival technique enthusiast. My friend Kacper (who is now an anthropologist) used to hunt for pigeons in the town centre of Poznań when he was still a student. Especially when he ran out of money towards the end of the month.

Of course there's a lot more food in the city, as proven by Poles who move to England and eat carp out of city ponds. There are not only pigeons, but also crows, rooks and jackdaws, which are delicious when they're young and soft, and unpleasant when old. Once upon a time, we would throw these birds into the pot, too.

There are also cats and dogs. Some guy who had escaped from prison once told me he fed on them. He preferred dogs. Cat fat was too liquid for his taste.

In cities one can always resort to looking through bins, especially near supermarkets and restaurants. Eating in this way is a real sport and it can suck people in. They call it *dumpster diving*. This way of getting food is a form of *freeganism* – eating everything that's free, that is, out of bins, leftovers, wild plants and animals. Collecting food left behind by large restaurants was my favourite game on the ferry between Dover and Calais, where I was on the lookout for freshly abandoned lunches. They were usually left behind by women. Men tend not to give up, and eat everything. Sadly my friend, who also practiced this sport, ended up catching hepatitis.

Now dumpster diving is a common place. When my older daughter did it for the first time as a literature and philosophy student in Glasgow, I was so proud of her! It's a shame that some people who claim to live close to nature are so dependent on leftovers from shops. What will they do if their expired banana supplies run out in their supermarket?

What about mice and rats? Well, you can always try. Personally, I've read too much about the whole arsenal of hantaviruses and other nasty things rodents spread. Maybe they are evolutionarily adapted to kill everything non-rodent. They are really tasty nevertheless. I tried rats in Laos, where they are a delicacy. But these were bamboo rats collected in field on the edge of the jungle.

Once, driving to Kraków, I forgot to take my documents, cards, and money. All I had with me were two of my books and just enough petrol to get to there. I decided to sell the books and return with the money I earned. When I got to Kraków, I started feeling hungry. I stood in line for soup for the homeless, which was a bit pointless, because the next moment I saw a tree – a Swedish whitebeam (*Sorbus intermedia*) covered in fruit. Then I found some other autumn berries in Planty Park. At noon, I found a some small coin in the lining of my jacket, bought a baguette, then sold the books and peacefully drove home.

The Indianists

Indianists are lovers of Indians – Europeans who are more Native American than Native Americans. Do you remember being six years old and playing Indians, wearing a headband around your head with two chicken feathers glued to it? What is the great phenomenon of the Plains Indians made up of? The fact that so many people are fascinated by them? The sense of their independence? Power? The heroism of their fighting? Europeans certainly feel in communion with the North American Indians' climate. They're not like the Pygmies or the Bushmen, who can wander round naked in temperatures that never fall below zero. The Lakota, Blackfeet, or Crow are hunters of wind-swept and ice-cold plains who hunt animals similar to the European.

Their masculinity certainly arouses the imagination of Europeans with a patriarchal, Indo-European history. However, they would be surprised to find that many Native American tribes were matrilineal, descending from the female ancestor, and women were in a better position than they were in Europe.

These idealised Native North Americans that tend to be lumped together in fact form dozens of tribes with dozens of languages. Their members are as different from each other as a Pole is from an Albanian, Georgian, or Basque person.

The Lakota Indians, like many other tribes, tolerated homosexuality. People with this sexual orientation were called *berdache.* They could choose whether to become warriors. They were allowed to remain in the camp as the wife of another warrior. They were considered perfectionistic and attentive to detail. Things well made were praised with the words that 'they were probably made by some berdache'. How far removed from the homophobic slurs we still hear around us.

The Plains Indians also had a tradition for seeking visions. Any self-respecting warrior would have gone on his own journey. He would not always succeed. Before his trip, he would clean himself in a sweat lodge. He would go to a holy place, for example some mountain top, make a bed of branches, and lie down on it. He wouldn't eat or drink for three or four days, until the verge of death. Then the ghosts and visions would arrive. Sometimes, to tempt the ghosts further, he would make an offering by cutting off his finger as if it were fishing bait.

The Indians truly believed in dreams and visions. Strong visions from dreams were enacted, told, brought to life. This is well-illustrated in the book *Black Elk Speaks*.

If I had to say what our modern civilization lacks most, what makes us most different from our primitive ancestors, I think I would choose its lack of vision-seeking. Hence the emptiness, the instinctive search for drugs as a vulgar way of experiencing primitive visionary rituals.

I once went to a gathering of Native American enthusiasts. I didn't bring a tipi with me, just a normal polyester tent. I mention this because the first question I was asked was about my tent. Those with tipis camped in the centre, those with shop-bought tents on the side. The latter formed something like a separate reserve of underdogs, onlookers, not-fully-Indians. They were carefully watched by the so-called Indian police. Some person took out a guitar and started quietly singing a Bob Dylan song by one of the fires. After a few minutes, the said policemen ran up and ordered them: 'Please stop! We don't play non-Indian music here!'. An Indianist in a poncho was sitting at the neighbouring fire, playing some Peruvian melodies on a pipe. No-one stopped her. It looks like the Incan vibe was less in conflict with the gathering than Dylan.

A Volkswagen Transporter drove up to the campsite. A guy in a plume stepped out. I made conversation with him, sending that I might be in the company of one of the veterans. 'Call me Siuqs,' he said. That was the norm. Half-naked guys in loincloths with strips of leather at the front and back and plumes or single eagle feathers setting up their tipis. And, with them, their wives and girlfriends in floral dresses or denim tops, carrying the shopping, gas bottles, and drums.

This incredible lack of Native American-looking women, preferably with bare breasts hanging down to their waist, really irritated me. It caused a kind of aesthetic dissonance. However, I do understand that the need to be dressed up as an Indian is a form of crypto-transvestism, in a wide sense of the word. Not transvestism in the sense that the man wants to be dressed up as a woman, but rather the kind in which the man wants to be dressed up and made up, strange, wearing feathers and beads. While women have managed to fight their way to many rights as to how they can dress, men are only just beginning to do it.

There was even a Native American at the gathering. Probably some honorary guest from tribe X. I caught sight of him as he drove into the parking lot. He got out of the car and looked at the campsite. Then sat down. He was shaking with laughter. After a moment, he realized that he'd been spotted by his hosts. He got up, adopted the grave expression of a chief, and casually dusted off his four-pack of beer.

Pretending to be Indians might seem childish and naive, but it's dead serious. It leads to tensions between what's Indian and not-Indian. Native American elders and medicine men write protests against the fact that the people who first slaughtered, disinherited, and enslaved their communities now appropriate their traditions. So the Native Americans are behaving in the opposite way to the Apostles of the Church, who would like nothing more than for the

Arabs, Chinese, and Papuans to accept the Bible and so destroy their own culture. Native Americans resemble the Jews, who treat their religion and culture as internal to their nation. Of course there are exceptions, Native Americans who 'carelessly' spread their traditions.

Of course, 'white people' tend to adopt the external, easy, and pleasant parts of the Native American culture: their dress, patterns, tipis. Some go further. They adopt ceremonies, but usually the pleasant ones, like the Indian sauna. Few embark on a hunt for visions involving a four-day fast from food and drink, preceded by making an offering (cutting off) of their finger.

The sweat lodge (Indian sauna) itself, *inipi* to the Lakotas, is a great example of intercultural dissonances and problems. The sweat lodge is, or was, part of the lifestyle of all tribes of North American Indians. Other than the mechanical aspects it has in common with the sauna – that is, heated stones with water poured onto them in a confined space – it had its own deep religious, magical, social, and health-related elements. As a shaman combines the characteristics of a priest, medicine-man, and scholar, the sweat lodge combines elements of the sauna, bathroom, church, and pub. It was, after all, used for cleansing in a wide sense of the term: for relaxation after hunting, to curing the sick or cleansing before a trip in search of visions.

Sweat lodge ceremonies were resisted by the U.S. government and, until recently, illegal. Abstinence from these rites not only had a negative effect on the morals of reserve inhabitants, but also had an impact on their health and level of hygiene.

Meanwhile, in the second half of the XX century, sweat lodge ceremonies became popular in some White circles, at first among Hippie and post-Hippie movements, then in the widely understood New Age.

Some were orthodox in their practice of the sweatlodge, conducting it in accordance with customs passed on from a specific tribe, staying true to these traditions out of respect for them or even out of fear of ghosts. Others inherited only the exterior form, that is, the sauna in a small wigwam, covered with for example blankets, into which hot stones are carried and then placed in a pit in the centre. Both the former and the latter faced criticism. The first were accused by many Native Americans of theft of their customs, while the latter were accused of treating the ceremony in a shallow, sport-like way.

I myself organise sweat lodges partly for sport, partly in the traditional sense. I believe I have the right to. First of all, because the Native Americans also took up a lot of our customs. Globalisation is globalisation. Now the idea of cultural appropriation is a big issue. People who dress as Native Americans and re-invent their rituals are accused of stealing from their native culture. I myself am not fond of plastic shamans making money of native rituals, but I was deeply inspired by Native American culture. I will say it aloud: I hate it when people go on about the fact we cannot take things from native cultures. It is true – for years, e.g. in the USA many of the rituals were illegal and people were persecuted for performing them. But I believe in the freedom of cultural exchange. If native people around the world choose to use the Internet and Latin alphabet, I choose to make my own vision quest, and to seek the guidance of Native American spirits.

I once read Raymond Bucko's book entitled *The Lakota Ritual of the Sweat Lodge*. He was a Catholic chaplain of the Lakota who described taking part in Lakota sweat lodges. The Native Americans themselves also modified their approach to the sweat lodge. Apparently, out of lack of firewood, they heat up stones by burning tyres. Secondly, even if members of different tribes are opposed to the transferral of their rituals, I treat this knowledge as something stolen consciosly. The true mystery shall remain a mystery. If someone somewhere once learned this and made it known to others, then they are responsible for it. Thirdly, I support the 'fruit' doctrine, that is, in the words of Jesus himself (Mt, 7, 16-20):

You will know them by their fruits. Do men gather grapes from thornbushes or figs from thistles? Even so, every good tree bears good fruit, but a bad tree bears bad fruit. A good tree cannot bear bad fruit, nor can a bad tree bear good fruit. Every tree that does not bear good fruit is cut down and thrown into the fire.

If I can see or feel that something gives good fruit or at least no bad fruit, I think I can do it. Another version of this doctrine is the Native American approach to dreams: dreams ought to be treated seriously. If someone dreamt something, they should enact it in waking life, and waking life will verify the force of the dream. This reminds me of the character in Nabokov's *Two leggings: the making of a crow warrior*, who dreamt of an alteration in the sweat

110

lodge ritual. The elders agreed to alter the ritual as long as it has a concrete positive result. It did. And so, having dreamt something up, we have the right to bring it into daily life, as long as we take responsibility for the fruits. I once had a dream about a sweat lodge taking place in between Polish birch trees, where I call the spirits of my forest. And besides, maybe I'm not at all escaping my own traditions but returning to them. On the territory of today's Ukraine, the ancient Scythians warmed themselves in canvas shelters propped up by poles with hot stones inside them. Admittedly, the Scythians sprinkled them with cannabis...

Pepa

Pepa was walking along Czerniakowska Street. It was a grey and gloomy day. 'It's just as well there's no sleet like they said on TV' – she thought, afraid that the cars rushing past her could splash dirty water onto her cream-coloured outfit. Pepa hated dirt. She had a clean, fragrant flat. She took care that it was never dusty – her thirteen year old son had an allergy, so the flat was hypoallergic, without carpets or rugs, with everything closed away in cupboards to prevent dust from gathering.

Pepa was glad that Warsaw was covered in tiles and concrete. She could walk with clean shoes. She remembered her suburban route to school. She had to clean her shoes nearly every day. Since childhood, she disliked villages and small towns. 'Life in such a hole seems unnatural to me', she once said. And she ended up in Warsaw, in which she was in her element. 'After all, people need other people'. She loved large shopping centres. Not that she bought much. She was a sensible and disciplined person. She had a time-consuming job but nearly every day she found an hour to have a quick look inside and had free Sundays. She liked the smell of these shopping centres, the perfume, the smell of coffee, the light, the warmth, everything within reach, people flickering by on the escalators.

She worked in a large company in a big office block. She did well there, despite being overloaded by work. She got on well with her boss and found it easy to fill in pointless tables, printouts of bank transfers, reply to emails with orders.

Her husband, Mariusz, was a true hunter. He dealt in cars. He would go to Germany and find amazing offers. Barely dented cars for a quarter of their value. His job gave him freedom, he claimed. He loved the constant travel and fact that he didn't have to go to work every day. The roadside prostitutes he would meet up with when stopping for a pee added meaning to his life. He liked it when they were Bulgarian or Ukrainian rather than Polish, because as he told his pal, it made him feel like a savage getting at another tribe. An unfulfilled exogamist.

Mariusz's knack for hunting also included fishing. He rarely had time for it, he maybe did it once a month. In that time, when Mariusz finally made it fishing, Pepa was visited by Dorota, an old friend from school. Pepa left her the key under the doormat, and when she came back from work, they left the house for the closest café. But the cafe was too crowded and they didn't feel like getting on the tram, so they decided to have a coffee at McDonalds. Of course if what they serve there can even be called coffee. Anyway they went for something. Maybe a milkshake.

Dorota was grey as a mouse, sort of chalky, pale, like most Poles... a bit stern and strange. Maybe because she was so anaemic herself, she had a passion for energy: different kinds of therapy, healing, exercises, ways of working with it. Once they sat down, she told Pepa: 'You know, it's an amazing coincidence. I was just reading in *Witch* magazine that the secret to McDonald's success lies in the construction of its logo and interiors in accordance with the rules of feng-shui. Even here, red and gold dominate – it's like an emperor's palace. That's why energy flows so well here, and it makes me feel like a sl..., I mean a prostitute, because I come here. Not even to eat. Just to sit here. I even once wrote a poem about it:

> *God since I've stopped going to your temples*
> *I would have lost hope*
> *if not for this submersion in the Big Mac of mankind.*

If I were to comment on her poem, I would tell her that it's simply the beginning of the new XXI-century version of the Apocalypse with McDonald playing the role of the Beast.

Meanwhile Dorota kept going: 'In that same issue of *Witch* some dowser wrote that McDonald has positive radiesthetic vibrations and they always hire a dowser to make sure there are no water veins. And they apparently add pheromones to their hamburgers. They have special dog farms in China where they suck the pheromones out of bitches in heat. Because the human ones are similar to dogs', foxes', or pine martens'. They just need a little chemical modification.'

Flow

I'm on the bus from Tarnów to Krosno, a two hour journey. It's packed and stinks of sweat. The driver cheerfully turns the steering wheel and waves his gearstick around. The drivers I usually encounter are much sadder and more frustrated. This one is really nice and beaming with happiness. Why is it that some people can be happy spending their lives as bus drivers while others cannot? What makes people so different? Is it what awaits them at home or some inner propensity for driving? Some people spend their whole lives on the same repetitive tasks and seem content. I once found myself working in an English slaughterhouse for a couple of weeks. I stood on the production line for eight hours a day, tearing off the skin of three thousand pig bellies each day. Sara, an English woman in her fifties, stood next to me, looking like a pink pig herself. It's a miracle they didn't turn her into sausages. She lived half a kilometer away from the slaughterhouse. I asked her how long she's been working on the production line. She said that she's been there her whole life, that is, since she left secondary school. 'I like it here' – she said. Meanwhile I could see the daffodils in bloom outside the slaughterhouse and nearly smell the grass. I wasn't happy.

As studies by Mihály Csíkszentmihályi have shown, people usually claim that they are most happy when in a state of 'flow', when their consciousness does not encounter too much resistance, their thoughts and actions move in accordance with their intentions and what they are interested in or in what isn't too difficult. It's best if it's something that's slightly engaging, like driving a car, working in an office, digging a ditch. Things like family and sex are, surprisingly, further back. They are an important part of a satisfied life, but in terms of the everyday sense of happiness, 'flow' is king.

What sense of flow did primitive people have? Time flew for them, so they probably experienced a lot of it. Women dug edible roots out of the forest floor as now they dig out potatoes. Men repaired their weapons or went hunting. There were some bad periods of hunger, illness, or sudden change of weather. Nevertheless, it's fascinating that people have such varied needs. Modern appliances often give us an opportunity to sink into a state of 'flow': driving a car, watching TV, spending time online. On the other hand, specialization is on the rise. We are expected to do only one thing: to be a secretary, driver, teacher, hairdresser. People used to walk to work or at least to the bus stop and had to stand in a packed bus. Now they drive and some muscles barely get used. Or even stay at home working using their laptops.

Primitive people were forced to and able to assume different roles and make a variety of movements that we rarely do: carrying heavy objects on their heads, kneeling down to excrete, sneaking up on prey, carrying a child on their backs, etc. And they danced a lot. I don't like dancing myself, but when I lecture I sit on the table and wave my legs around. And sometimes I crawl round the house for a change of perspective.

Hunting

115

I think the element of the primitive lifestyle of my ancestors that I would find hardest to imitate would be being a true hunter. I don't like killing animals and have a weak reflex and no stamina. I've eaten fish, frogs, and lizards that I've caught myself. I've eaten roadkill and birds that fell out of their nests. However, I've not mastered the art of killing larger animals. Once upon a time, when I still thought I'd learn to hunt someday, in the first year of my living in my village, I went on a very long walk along a ridge overgrown by beech trees. I could see myself with a bow and arrow, hunting stags. It was so tangible. Then suddenly... suddenly I saw a deer lying on the ground. No movement. It was warm. It had a wound on its upper body, it had been shot. Poachers, I thought. I hid in the thicket and waited to see what happened next. After half an hour I decided to take the deer. I'm not sure what tempted me. I decided that the fact that I'd spotted the deer gave me the right to decide its fate. This lost shot deer was a gift from Providence to me. I slung it over my shoulder. It was heavy. I decided to drag it along the ravine, then hide it and take it back home in pieces (but how?) in my backpack. The large mass terrified me. How do I cut it? I'd always wanted to gut a deer, to learn how to quickly and efficiently divide the skin, organs, and different parts of its flesh. Here was my chance to supplement my diet nettle soups with deer goulash.

So I dragged it through the woods for over a mile. Then I heard a voice: 'Stop, or we'll shoot you!'. I was surrounded. Thirty hunters in combat clothes and hats with a feather on top. 'Where are you from?'. 'Pietrusza Wola' – I said (I think they were from the neighbouring village). They didn't believe me. I was new and they didn't know who I was. 'Don't fuck with us and say you're from Pietrusza Wola you cunt, just give us the deer and get the fuck out of here or we'll shoot you.'

I got the chance to gut a deer a few years later. My sister was directing a film in the Łagiewniki Forest in Łódź, for which she needed game to lie in the snow. She bought one. It didn't have entrails but it was still a lot of work cutting it! My neighbour Piotr began doing it the Native American way. He spoke to the dead deer, apologised for its death, and placed a little tobacco in its mouth.

Karma[20]

It was a beautiful July day. The builders were just putting up the scaffolding to renovate the local church. They made their way further and further up with their planks of wood. Sometimes they came down to us to get water from the well. That day, too, one of them appeared at my house, this time without a bottle in his hand.

'Take it!' – the worker held four bloody birds in his hand. Three of them were dead but still warm, and one, with a smashed head and deformed leg, was still twitching.

'Why me?'

'Cause I heard you eat everything. Shame to waste it. They fell out of their nest.'

'Give them to me.' I said.

I laid them out on a board. I slashed the twitching one with a knife to spare it the suffering. They barely had any

---

[20] In Polish *karma* also means food for animals.

feathers. It only took one pull to remove their skin. I skewered them. Yum.

It's natural, not snobbish, to seek diversity. We are drawn to things that are new, exceed our previous experiences, draw us to them. Fear of the new is there, but if we open our senses to the full experience: food, travel, sex, the craving to go further and more always arises. You have to know how to stop.

My neighbour once came and said: 'Wanna buy a bat?'

'What would I need a bat for?' I asked.

'You buy everything, I figured you'd think of something. Maybe you'll eat it or dry it or sell it in Warsaw. I know ya, you'll make something out of it.'

I felt the brief temptation to eat the bat. Then I remembered that they can carry rabies, and their black fur, their small bones, and the laws for animal protection. Just in case, I asked for the price, just to know the current market price of a bat in my region.

'Well... two wines.'

'Too much.' I said.

'Too much?'

His eye for business also made itself known in him: 'You see, a bat has two wings so I deserve two wines.'

'Here's one and let it go.'

'All right. No-one else would buy it anyway.'

And whoosh, the bat flew under the roof of my house.

That's when I remembered how I was told as a child that bats are sent down by the devil. As recently as towards the end of the XX century, some inhabitants of Krosno caught them, dried them, and hung them up in their attics as a kind of amulet.

118

Back then I was unaware that in a few years I would find out that people in some run-down regions of Indochina eat bats. I missed such a great chance. When I went to Thailand in 2008 I could not find it in market. I asked for bat goulash in vain. They told me it's only eaten in one region of the country, the one I didn't manage to get to. And it's also possible to contract all sorts of diseases from it. The youths definitely don't want to eat bats. I told this story to my international students from the Warsaw International Studies in Psychology. A student from Ghana raised her hand. They told me that bats are widely eaten in their region, too.

But I was happy to taste them eventually in Laos, ten years later. I bought a four-pack of bats, with legs tied with a pieced wood bark. I brought them to a culinary course in one of the cooking schools in Luangrabang and asked them to teach me how to make it. First they grilled the animals and then wrapped it in a banana leaf and steamed it for nearly two hours. It was delicious!

I've been brought not only bats, but sometimes other fairly fresh demonic animals that met tragic deaths which assured me of their freshness: lizards cut in half by lawnmowers or grass snakes run over by cars. Once a guy turned up in my cabins' doorway with a 1.5 m long grass snake. He just killed it. He kept it in his hand with tweezers. It was a fat female. When I cut its guts, a gigantic, freshly swallowed toad came out. It was like the picture of a snake who swallowed an animal from *The Little Prince*. When I cut further down 36 eggs came out. I had a dozen of boiled snake eggs for three day in a row.

Albert

Albert was interested in Chinese medicine. He kept repeating that I eat moist foods, that I need to dry out because my body has gathered up too much water. He once visited me while I was building a new shelter made of branches and grass in my forest. To be fair, he didn't just go on and on about his medicine, but also helped me with carrying branches.

'Why not buy some fabric for the tipi?'

'Because I want it to be natural. They make tipis in factories, you know, out of imported string.'

'Well, I like the canvas... Besides, the grass you're collecting here comes from the meadow, not the forest. Meadows aren't natural, only forests are.'

'But it's organic.' I defended. 'This cone construction, a few poles tied together and covered with dry grass is probably mankind's most primitive kind of cottage.'

'The most primitive, but not that great, ha, ha.' Albert attacked. 'Look, these poles making up the construction are going to have a negative energetic effect on you. And the cone-like shape, according to the Chinese, takes away people's *yang* energy.'

'Maybe you're right, a semi-circular wigwam does have a nicer shape. But it's a shame it takes so much longer to make...'

Albert was always one of the most natural people I knew. There was nothing that made him stand out, but he was wise and calm. And very slow. You could see the way in which he considered every thought in fifty combinations. As an astrological Taurus, he knew what he wanted.

Once, sitting with him by the fire, I began to wonder what all of my friends have in common. Among them, there are professors and vagabonds, professional schizophrenics, businessmen and lumberjacks. Then I understood. They didn't work regularly. I mean, they did work, but only from time to time, or when they wanted to, or three days a week (a scientist has to work…), but they didn't have a 9-5. Let's call things what they are – they weren't slaves.[21]

A chief of the Nez Perces tribe once explained his reasons for refusing to adopt a normal Western way of life: 'My sons aren't going to work, their dreams would lose their power.'

So maybe I surround myself with people whose dreams are powerful? Maybe. Personally, I consider dreams to be a great gift, and awareness of them and connection with them to be a basis of spiritual development, the beginning of one's unity with oneself and the cosmos. It's interesting that I've had the most vivid dreams when living in Warsaw, in a small, nearly empty room, in a grey block of flats. My move to the countryside, surprisingly, perhaps temporarily (for fourteen years now…), scattered this dream potential in me. Or maybe I've already fulfilled it. Maybe it's better to dream less? Not that I dreamt awfully intensely back in Warsaw. There was a lot of running through empty hills covered with sheep fescue and all sorts of flowers, depending on the day: ragged robins, crocuses, gentians. It was the ragged robin that called me in my Warsaw dreams, shouting: 'Come back to us, to the meadows, to the hills'. In

---

[21] Here my Polish version editor Ania Wojciechowska, who works as a full-time teacher, added: 'And me? :-)'

that empty room with white walls and a green floor, in the grey block of flats, looking at the lights of the tramline, I dreamt that mountains had surfaced on the other side of the Vistula river, in the Praga quarter. They were made of increasingly tall cliffs, like those you see in the Kraków area. A dreamy union of Kraków with Warsaw. I spent those years searching for natural places in Warsaw. They're there. Lost somewhere between crossroads. I'd go to Cwil's Hill at night, which was heaped up while the Ursynów estate was being built. It has the shape of a zikkurat. I'd often sit there between 10 p.m. and midnight. There were usually some people with their dogs. Why didn't anyone else want to sit at the top? Cars went around me and lights flickered through flat windows. Maybe they were waiting for me to get down to take their solitary spots? Then there was the Vistula, a wild, beautiful river. I remember Sarah's birthday when we built fires on the ice and I read her *The Little Prince*.

Fish

When I hear someone being called a *wild person*, I hear the words of the actor Daniel Olbrychski in *Colonel Wolodyjowski*. 'I am Asia Tuchajbejowicz'. I can hear him tear apart his shirt and show his symbol – fish tattooed onto his chest, a picture on the body, the first human clothing. A tattoo is already derivative. First there was covering yourself with clay and ash. Painting breasts with mushed wild strawberries and raspberries. Drawing circles and spirals on the torso with charcoal. Smearing the face with blood. Painting a yellow line on the nose. Since I started writing this book ten years ago, the tattoo trend has been on the rise. There's a whole new generation of tattooed men and women.

Embers

Humans can walk on fire. Not strictly on fire but on embers. You light a big fire from branches or chips of wood, and once it burns down to a small heap of reddened nut-like coals like nuts, you scatter them. And anyone, nearly everyone, can run across them. It's hard to believe but it's true. There's still no good physical explanation for it. There must be some layer of insulation in our feet, because after all, a hand placed on such hot embers would burn, not to mention knees or calves.

So we have feet immune to embers. We are, then, not just water apes, children of rivers and oceans, born like hippopotamuses and dolphins to explore aquatic pantries. We're also the children of the pagan gods of lighting, fire, and conflagration. We probably used to run across burned-down, still-smoking forests and savannahs, over the hot ash, gathering half-carbonised antelopes. Maybe we discovered this gift further along. The ritual of walking on embers still exists in some cultures in southern Asia, in Hawaii, in different secret Islamic brotherhoods, and as for Europe, among the Bulgarians.

In Bulgaria, the custom of walking on embers is called Anastenaria. The Nestinari step onto the embers with religious icons. This ritual most often takes place on the feast day of Constantine and Elena at the end of May. It has survived in a few villages in the Strandzha Mountains of southeastern Bulgaria.

I was taught to walk on embers by Wojciech Jóźwiak. He is a Polish astrologist, thinker and New Age shaman. We would collect a large pile of branches cut up into small chips, as if for a stove. Once the flames were gone and the pile would begin to burn down and consisted of orange, hot, nut-sized embers, we would scatter these embers and line them up into a path a few metres long, then walk on it. I was really scared the first time and I'm still always a bit scared. Making a few steps on embers seems to be against human nature, something totally magical, impossible, and perverse. Not everyone is scared. Some even dance on the embers.

Wojtek's workshops, during which he organises walks on embers, are very serious and form a certain liturgical whole. The fire is given offerings to and spoken to. And, God forbid, no-one drinks beer. The participants – I guess – think that if they stepped on fire after a beer, the fire would consume them whole.

Meanwhile, I was witness to an ember-walking ritual initiated with beer. The Wzdów Institute of Folk Culture would burn a large wicker man every year on summer solstice. The burning embers form a large circle which is very tempting to step into. I saw people walk into it, enthused by the music, after five cans of Warka beer and having no idea how to walk on fire. It's not without reason that Pope Clemens called out on his deathbed: '...sancta piva di Polonia... sancta biera di Warka...'.

Smell

We lost our sense of smell before we became humans. Like monkeys, we're very visual. But smell is still there and those who use it go far. We take smell away from our children. We stupefy them with the visual, sometimes with sound. They're more rarely offered touch. What about smell? Do children have a single hour in the week devoted to smell education? Only the blind experience it out of necessity. Our natural forest food doesn't differ too much from what wild boar eat. And a wild boar knows how to sniff it out. Countless rows of acorns I planted were eaten away by wild boar. They stopped doing it when I covered them with smelly elderflower branches. By then, they had eaten so many rhizomes of bittercresses…

There's a lot a human can sniff out – it is, to a large extent, only a matter of training. Of dividing things into their smaller components. I already know what a rat smells like. I can sniff it out in a barn. And I know the smell of a fox, of rotting alders and oaks. Beech leaves smell different. There are forests that smell of raspberries and those that smell of blackberries. Some stink of nettles. And lawns we walk on first let out the fresh smell of thyme, a pharmaceutical whiff of St John's wort, and further along they smell of wet hair, of fescue. You keep walking and smell the earth from a fresh molehill and the feathers of a dead wood pigeon.

Silt in the stream reeks of ferric oxide. Bubbles of gas come out of the source. The bog-spring smells of cowslip, horsetail, and valerian. You step three metres further into the mud and are surprised by the aspirin aroma of meadowsweet rhizomes and the clove-and-mud fragrance of wood avens.

At first these smells might be hard to separate. But slowly you begin to learn what smells, where it smells, and how it smells. What helped me was collecting plants for their seeds. When drying a stack of only one species at a time in my attic, I could learn the smell of each individual species in depth and in detail. Sometimes the whole attic would smell of ragged robins, other times of evening primrose, oxeye daisies, or St. John's wort. Ragged robins and oxeye daisies have a calming effect similar to camomile. It soothes the soul to be around it. Evening primrose also smells sweet with a slight aroma of vanilla, like the body of a young olive-skinned girl. The ragged robin is similar, but you also get a note of perfume. As for brown knapweed – it hits you with its rigid and calm bitterness. And betony arouses you and clears your mind. No wonder it was used against headaches.

Leaves

'The Pirahã don't eat leaves,' – a Pirahã Indian said at the sight of the anthropologist Daniel Everett eating salad – 'why do you?'. Leaves are an important subject. Many societies are somewhat averse to them, treating them as something only for wrapping up meat and roots for roasting. Other societies treasure them and believe they give them health. They cut them up and eat them raw, stir fry or cook them. Gorillas eat mainly leaves, while chimps consume much less.

126

Slavs mostly ate sorrel, goosefoot and nettle, which form the soup Holy Trinity for all Slavs. Other leaves are less popular and associated with impoverishment, preharvest, and famine.

One of the leaves associated with times of hunger is *Cirsium rivulare*, a soft thistle common on Carpathian meadows. It used to save highlanders from hunger. 'Good but makes you fart', they used to say. I tried it. It tastes like slightly bitter lettuce and indeed, when I gave my students some to try the whole group ended up farting away happily.

After eating leaves, your excrement looks healthy and dark brown. Sometimes it's even green. And it doesn't stick, so you use less paper. If you eat too many of them – if you eat nothing else – it will begin to become runny and you'll get diarrhoea from eating only this kind of stuff. That is what the people from the Qinling Mountains told me about the Great Famine of China (1959-61).

During a famine in the Kurpie region, its inhabitants ate a lot of nettle. They picked it all day, cooked it and ate it, and by evening they were hungry again. I tried this out wandering through the forest. You keep eating linden leaves all day, you reach the volume of a bucketful and only just start feeling slightly satisfied. A Carpathian villager once said to an ethnographer: 'When there was famine, that's when we ate, thistles. Enough to fill a barn. And we were still hungry.'

Adrenal glands

The life of our primeval ancestors was far from rosy. One of the worst things that could happen was being accused of hexing someone. This happened in many cultures. In modern courts, the culprit needn't be found. It used to be acceptable to select someone in place of the criminal. At night, the Australian Aborigines cut the adrenal glands from their victims accused of witchcraft. In others, only the fear of a hex antidote being performed on them by a witch doctor caused death or illness. Douglas Lockwood provides a colourful description of this in his book *I, The Aboriginal.*

Fishermen

Fishermen are an underappreciated relict group of hunter-gatherers. You'd think they're just Boring Guys with Beers, sitting on the riverbank with their fishing rods, but they are a source of ancient wisdom, hunting artistry and experiences equal to those of primitive warriors. They can distinguish between dozens of species of fish. They know what they look like, taste like, how they move and when they breed. They know where they find food, spend the winter, heatwaves, and times of rain. They also know what they like to eat. They know of every single worm that fish find tasty. I was never quite able to fully grasp this craft. I gave too much of myself to plants. Although I do participate in fishing from time to time, it's not the same. As a pragmatist, I am more drawn to catching fish with nets, hands, or to using poison. Fishing feels suspiciously like an ideology or a calling.

But jokes aside – the fishermen's ways resemble the lifestyle of primitive humans. First of all, they mostly catch wild food. Secondly, they catch all sorts of things using their knowledge about their environment. They don't do anything tiring – they just sit there and catch.

I nearly became a fisherman. I grew up two hundred metres away from the Wisłok river. My mum didn't let me go to the river alone, but I would sneak out and meet up with my friends who were obsessed with fishing. It's a shame they didn't eat their catch. Their mums told them that the fish were contaminated, so they caught them for pure enjoyment and to give them to their cats to eat. Better than nothing. Besides, they were usually just bleaks, gudgeons, sometimes small roaches, more rarely barbels or chubs.

This year, a day after I finished my workshops after a few days of cooking meals made of wild plants, I sat down with a neighbour from a nearby village at a civilised bonfire by the river Wisłok. Another guest joined the party. He says: 'I caught fifty chubs today'. And true enough, he started taking out fish after fish. Beautiful, with red fins, like some Amazonian characids. Already cleaned. He laid them down on the grill above the fire. I don't think I've ever been so jealous of anything in my life. Not of their meat, of course. I can eat as much as I want. I was jealous of the experience of a great hunt. I felt the jealousy of a warrior whose fellow tribesman has killed fifty bison.

Limits

When writing about wildness and naturalness in this book, on the one hand I present people who transcend the limits of modern, Western 'normality', who are often considered freaks but whose behaviour could be described as stereotypical or boring in other societies. I also write about different societies, relicts of the past, of prehistory. Can we consider any custom of the past 'natural'? Yes and no. Whether they like it or not, people, as biological creatures, are always a part of nature, so in some sense, they are always 'natural'. But I wanted to present modal naturalness. Just the way that statistics show how much the average person earns, I wanted to show what an average natural person looks like, and what the average return to nature might be.

The world 'wild' can be problematic. On one hand, we might associate it with epithets such as *close to nature, out of control, independent, organic,* on the other hand with adjectives such as: *cruel, unbridled, predatory, bloodthirsty, ruthless, immoral.* The exploration of this second set of epithets would have to involve a description of the most sadistic crimes, both individual and collective. I won't do this, but we ought to be aware of this aspect of human nature, of the cruelty of a boy chopping wings off flies and of what happened in Auschwitz. It is not too far from one to the other.

The wild are only wild sometimes

If we were to make a 'Flintstones' theme park, where we could take our family for the weekend or, even better, go for a trip together with co-workers from your company and see a real/pretend wild person, and if I described this to you, most likely the first thing you would imagine would be people dressed in skins or naked, hunting for large animals, bloody initiation rituals, flights between tribes, dances and tam-tams. These are the kinds of scenes we might expect to see in films like 'Quest for Fire'. However, the everyday life of wild people might actually turn out to have been quite boring. It would resemble family life from our own home or scenes from shows such as 'Big Brother'. Gossip, children pretending to be adults, digging in the soil for roots, picking berries. Men returning from hunts tired just like after a full day's work. Smiles, smiles like ours, although as psychologists and anthropologists stress, more frequent than in our times. And packing the camp up is the equivalent of moving house or going away on holiday. I think the structuralists were right to stress the unity of human culture. What we find wild and different reveals itself from time to time. In everyday life, the wild are not wild, they are people.

Ishi

Ishi is the last uncivilized Native American in Northern California. Ishi is not his real name, but the word for human in his language. Ishi was born sometime in the mid XIX century (around 1860) and died in 1916. He was found by a group of men in the village of Oroville in 1911. The Yahi tribe of the Yana group, like many other tribes of its time, fell prey to the gold fever in California. In 1865 it was nearly entirely massacred, with the exception of a few dozen people. Finally, from all the people living in an increasingly civilised California, hiding for dozens of years from the whites, only Ishi survived. He lived the solitary existence of a real hunter-gatherer for many years, hunting for game and collecting wild plants. When he was found, he was in a bad state, very thin, in rags. His discovery caused a sensation and aroused great interest. He was moved to the University of California in Berkeley, where he lived in a building that belonged to the Museum of Anthropology. Two researchers, Alfred L. Kroeber and Thomas Talbot Waterman, took him under their care. Slowly, they reconstructed his language, and Ishi gave them valuable anthropological information about the life of his tribe. Kroeber's wife, Theodora, published a book entitled *Ishi in Two Worlds*. Ishi died of tuberculosis in 1916.

When asked what he enjoyed most in white people's culture, Ishi replied that he liked bathrooms and running water (which were, of course, more available in America than in Europe at the time). He was fascinated by the possibility of having his own 'private stream' at home. However, he hated the city and crowds.

Maybe if he were alive today he'd say, 'I love bathrooms and the Internet', and still hate the city.

Wild boar

Why are wild boar in my book? Well, in the words of the Polish children's poet Jan Brzechwa, 'A wild boar's wild'. So let's go with it. Besides, the wild boar likes what people like. Its treats – acorns, grubs, and forest plants such as lesser celandine or toothwort, are also food fit for human consumption that our ancestors in fact fed on.

Brzechwa wrote: 'The wild boar is wild, the wild boar is evil'. Wildness is associated with evil. I think it has been for a long time now. In many mythologies, the wild boar is

132

the ruler of the dark part of nature. A chtonic animal of primeval forests and swamps. It digs in the ground, it stinks, it's not afraid of carrion.

Tearing off

The fascination with wildness is grounded in part in a fascination with simplicity and nostalgia for moving away from unnecessary dependencies, details, surpluses or entanglements. A hunter-gatherer often had only their close ones, maybe some weapons or a utensil they were still able to make themselves from the materials surrounding them, ridding themselves of things they didn't need, such as shirts. Like the Hutsul who wore fur over his naked body. Sahlins called this the economy of Zen.

However, we often forget that people of the wild were caught up in their own ecosystem and spirit world. They belonged to their land. They knew only the plants and animals of their land. If moved a few hundred kilometres away, they could struggle to survive. Wild humans had their places of power, places where their ancestors rested; they had their favourite camping spots and springs. They had their favourite fruit trees they'd go back to. Holy mountains. Especially friendly beaches. It's part of human nature to get caught up in things. By stripping away some, we are in danger of getting caught up in others.

The health food shop

The health food shop is Mekka for people in search of a natural lifestyle. It's a spot haunted mainly by women, firstly because they tend to take better care of their health, and secondly because they more frequently stick to a vegetarian diet, and it's especially vegetarians who purchase their products there. Products labelled as WITHOUT sugar, WITHOUT preservatives, ORGANIC, BIO, ECOLOGICAL, BIOLOGICAL, BIODYNAMIC, etc., are an expression of people seeking natural products. However, it turns out that the shop can also be a place not only for those in search of the natural, but also those who are looking for the wild. Here you can find pasteurised birch sap, acorn coffee, acorn flour or wild rice (*Zizania aquatica*), a grain that is wild by its very name, as it could not be tamed and has managed to resist mass production. Today it grows just like it did centuries ago by the Great Lakes of North America. It used to feed Native American tribes and today it feeds tribes of seekers of healthy food. Customers of health food shops actually belong to a few distinct tribes: vegetarians out of love for animals, orthorexics (people who are obsessed with healthy eating), people with conditions such as diabetes and diseases of the circulatory system, and finally seekers of new tastes, for whom an increasing amount of stores with exotic or oriental foods are currently emerging. I myself belong to the latter group and usually avoid health food shops and opt for oriental stores. I've made a definitive move away from them after one spring during which I saw people buying pasteurised birch sap from the previous year when the forests were already bursting with fresh sap.

'Puszta' and 'puszcza'

If you ask people what they associate with wildness, some will describe deserts, others – places filled with wild animals and plants. In our country, the wildest place is the primeval forest, especially the Wildest of the Wild – the Białowieża Forest (more specifically, its centre, as the rest has been turned into a wood factory). The source of the Polish word for the primeval forest – 'puszcza' – is a confusing term related to the word for emptiness. It is only empty in the sense of having no people in it, but of course it is full of absolutely everything that is not human. The 'puszta' – the Hungarian grassy steppe– is more empty than the 'puszcza', but the etymology is the same – the Slavic term for emptiness.

If we counted the species in the primeval forest we would come up with a big number. But the largest amount of species inhabits the border of forest and non-forest. For centuries, humans have been enriching nature by cutting down the forest. There used to be so much forest that the fields we formed were like oases in the desert – places filled with sun-loving flowers and insects.

Then the situation turned around. Primeval forests became islands surrounded by fields, meadows, and pastures, which thanks to fertilisers, herbicides and pesticides have recently become wastelands in terms of their flora and fauna. Fifty or a hundred years ago the meadows and pastures were filled with flowers and butterflies despite, and often thanks to, the fact they were mowed and grazed. The eighteenth century was a time of the greatest biological diversity in Poland. Forests were still

135

rarely monocultures, meadows and pastures were teaming with plant species such as meadow saffron, carline thistle and gladiolus which are rare nowadays, and some foreign species from America had been introduced as well. Today, floristic impoverishment in my region of the world occurs mainly because species die out in hay meadows and dry pastures due to turbulent changes in uses of the land.

Workshops

While trying to run away from civilization, I quickly understood the deception behind my dream. Or maybe it didn't happen so quickly, but after a year or two. For a good few years since moving to the countryside, I felt guilty about my lack of energy to realise my dream about wildness and self-sufficiency. Sitting at home, I'd think about it more or less once an hour, seeing myself hunched up in a shelter, not sitting on the sofa by the fire. Only when the temperature fell below ten degrees Celsius would these doubts somehow disappear. Trying to understand my drive to thinking about being There, in the forest, rather than Here, by the fire, I understood it was not only a question of wildness, but of the fact I felt some general sorrow about the human condition. About the fact we're not like a dog or a stag, a creature that can live self-sufficiently, moving between the indoors and the outdoors without taking off or putting on shoes and coats. A being that never takes a bag with it, that doesn't know money or forks. Of course, it's possible to find individuals close to my ideal among people – tramps, the homeless, the mad, the saints (here I recommend Jacek Sieradzan's fantastic monograph *Szaleństwo w religiach świata* [*Madness in Religions of the World*]), but one must admit that such a life is exceedingly difficult for humans living outside a (sub)tropical climate. Probably my guests who don't change their clothes for a few days at a time come the closest to this ideal.

But let's return to my main train of thought. To what happened next, when I failed...

I began to build shelters on my land, in a field. I'd sleep in them sometimes, especially in the winter, when I felt more of a need to be 'outdoors'. Sometimes different friends would turn up and we'd camp together, collect wild plants, build the next shelters, start fires with a bow drill, and sit around.

At first, it was non-commercial. More and more people started coming but I always wanted our meetups to be contained. You come, we spend a few days together, and you leave. I learned the value of this when I took part in Wojtek Jóźwiak's workshops, where there is perfect unity of time, place, and action. Wojtek doesn't even let latecomers into his workshops. Workshops and meetups become a kind of communal theatre. Meanwhile, our meetings were chaotic. Sometimes there were meant to be twelve people and only one would arrive, so I introduced a registration fee and it worked. People started arriving on time, and always at least half of those who registered would turn up. And, worst of all, it started making us money. That's how something Paleolithic became a business – a really pleasant business which I still treat in a quasi-religious way. I treat my own workshops as if I was myself showing up in someone else's space, as if I were leaving home. It's a celebration of the time of year. If they take place in spring, they're a celebration of spring, in summer – a celebration of summer. The same place can be very different. People who come at different times of year find themselves in a different place. Workshops which at first concerned general survival skills – in which we would eat, build, and practice different techniques – became cooking workshops or as they call them foraging workshops. It just happened. Wild food is the only thing I know a lot about. I'm happy that different kinds of people are drawn to my workshops. I've had company managers, students of biology, ethnology, food technologies and IT, a sausage quality inspector, whole hoards of pharmacists, a health food shop assistant, a dentist, a student of Russian, an academic and editor of baking magazine in one, a punk-potter from Germany, hippies from all over, a few dozen scouts, servicemen, a judge, visual artists, etc., etc.. I haven't yet encountered a priest, mathematician, or car mechanic.

Meetings to do with wild cooking induce a strange state in people. They're in nature, but not alone. Far from home, but cosy in straw tipis. Smoke-swept, squatting, laughing, their fingers soiled with clay after peeling marsh woundwort rhizomes, they seem exceptionally full to me – with their laptops hidden at the bottoms of their bags, with supplies of chocolate stashed away, they are at least a little stripped of the excess of civilization.

Washing and not washing

Today, some of us associate the wild with dirt or lack of hygiene. But when Europeans first came across the native inhabitants of North America, it was the opposite. It was the Europeans who avoided washing and wore dirty, sweated-through cloth and leather clothing, while the Native Americans regularly washed themselves in the river. Besides, the hygienically cleansing ritual of the Native American sauna was one of their society's key events. Early medieval thermal baths were popular in European cities. Despite the low level of hygiene, people happily went to the baths, also for social reasons. People weren't too ashamed of their bodies. Then waves of epidemics came along and limited human contact. Bathing and the baths became something dangerous. Dirt fell off on its own or remained on clothing. The whole XVIII and XIX centuries were times of great dirt. Steam rooms and saunas survived only in the coldest countries, where they soothed the cold and discomfort of winter.

For different people, a return to nature can serve both as initiation to dirt, a way of releasing themselves from their fear of dust, bacteria, and mud. For others, a trip to the sea or the river – an ablution in the wet parts of nature – will count as such a return instead.

Betel

One of the main characteristics of the mind-altering substances – today vulgarly called 'drugs' or 'stimulants' – used by primitive people was the fact that they grew locally. Sometimes they were rare, like the European belladonna but local nevertheless. I became aware of this when chewing betel – a mild stimulant used by inhabitants of southern Asia. In Thailand and Malaysia the *Areca catechu* palms, the nuts of which are the main ingredient of this substance, grow everywhere, while betel pepper (*Piper betle*) can be found in the forest. Other than areca nuts and pepper, ingredients of the chewed mix include spices and limewash. Betel has a stimulating, slightly bewildering effect – something between having a coffee and getting tipsy on beer on a hot day. Like most traditions, the use of psychoactive plants has its good and bad sides. Good, because it refreshes and disinfects the digestive system, working toxically on many parasites. Bad, because in the long run, it causes the blackening and falling out of teeth. It also increases the likelihood of contracting certain diseases – worst of all, it significantly increases the chances of developing some types of stomach cancer. In Thailand, it is the stimulant of choice chiefly for elderly female villagers. When I ask to taste betel in a village, everyone laughs... The use of betel is somehow limited to tropical and subtropical regions of Asia and Madagascar and exists there already – it grows there wild or is easy to grow. it's a natural stimulant, a local, regional product.

Why didn't fly agaric, *Amanita muscaria*, the hero of illustrations in children's books and the sacred mushroom of Siberian tribes, which gives their shamans sacred visions, become a local product to us? A ritualistic soup? An ingredient in a sacred stew? Many people who have experimented with it trace this back to the unpleasant sensations such as nausea and vomiting that accompany visions. Yesterday I spoke to someone who ate six caps and nearly fell into a coma. In Siberian tribes people drank the urine of those who ate the mushrooms. Drinking such urine doesn't involve any side effects. Maybe the Slavs weren't aware of this?

Why was another local product – mushrooms from the *Psilocybe* genus – unknown to Europeans? These small mushrooms often grow in pastures on rainy autumn days. There used to be more such pastures but the use of mushrooms only became widespread along with hippie culture. Maybe Christianity is to blame for this. Over the last thousand years there has been no lack of magicians, witches, and simple village shepherds in search of new experiences. But the passage of traditional knowledge from real experts was destroyed by witch hunts and inquisition. The Białystok ethnobotanist Ewa Pirożnikow encountered traces of a tradition of children in the Podlasie region eating a plant they called *durna repka* (literally 'mad raddish'): the seeds of henbane (*Hyoscyamus niger*) or datura (*Datura stramonium*). Children would bite them apart with a passion, while their parents reprimanded them whenever they noticed that their child was on 'durna repka'.

In the Carpathians, the most popular natural psychoactive was probably belladonna (*Atropa belladonna*). This plant is common in fields adjacent to beech woods. It was worshipped in Romania (where it was known under the name of *matraguna*, after its mandragora cousin). Mircea Eliade vividly described customs related to its use in his book *De Zalmoxis à Gengis-Khan. Études comparatives sur les religions et le folklore de la Dacie et de l'Europe orientale*. It was the plant of life and death. It could bring good luck but also catastrophe. It was an ambivalent, unruly ally like the great many that can be found between the pages of books by Carlos Castaneda's, who was a famous propagator of hallucinogens.

And finally there is bog bilberry (*Vaccinium uliginosum*). It was considered poisonous and avoided in many Polish villages but picked in others. Sometimes eating it in large amounts causes intoxication similar to that resulting from alcohol. I didn't quite believe it until a few years ago. I ate two plates in a bog near Supraśl, and after a moment I was able only to walk on all fours. However, it didn't last long.

While we're at walking on all fours... it used to be my childhood dream. At the age of three, I had long phases of wanting to be someone other than a little boy, which some readers will no doubt be familiar with. I tried to be, among other things, a girl and a bird. I sat on chicken eggs that I stole from the chicken hatch for hours on end in vain. But I also tried to be somewhat like a cat or a dog (or maybe more like a baboon?).

Many lovers of going back to nature are enthusiasts of psychedelics. I agree with Terrence McKenna (1946-2000) that psychedelic mushrooms and plants may have pushed the development of human religion and mind forward. I am very sensitive to reality and have even experienced shamanic trance myself without chemical stimuli, so I do not normally practice the psychedelic path. But the one and only time I took LSD when I was 23 deeply affected my life. I travelled down inside me. I even saw my future land on which I now live, and it helped me to make the decision to quit my university job in Warsaw. And it helped me to reconnect with my inner child from the times I sat on eggs in my nest.

Seminar

I am attending a scientific botanical seminar in Białowieża. After thirteen years of trying to live in a shelter and discard civilization, I wonder what draws me to these people with their Power Point presentations with tables and talk about competition between species or the distribution of some rare flower.

Human gatherings are something natural. The desire to be not only with people who are our closest relatives are one of our most primitive needs. Why – if I add up my trips away from home to conventions, meetings and conferences – do the botanical ones dominate, rather than those under the slogan of *hey, let's go back to nature!*

Most meetups and gatherings of 'alternative' people are pretty boring. Of course, not immediately. Besides, botanical meetings can also be boring, a – for most people, b – after some time. The naturalness of the meeting results from the impulse of people wanting to meet. Scientific meetups can have many tribal features. Evenings, dance elements, meetings of elders, initiation, and the presentations and lectures themselves are the centre of the rite.

Botanists differ from one another. My conference roommate arrived at the conclusion that meetings of botanists specialised in land plants or vascular plants are rigid– it's a large group of botanists in which the older members stick together while the young stay separate. Bryologists' (moss specialists) meetups are different. The seminars are small and everyone spends time together. Apparently algologists (algae specialists) also drink a lot. Zoologists drink even more. Maybe the beings they study are their holy totems that they themselves become similar to. The land plant botanists, slow and anaemic, are a heavily stratified group, just like the plants they study, which include both big trees and small flowers. Then there are the egalitarian, modest bryologists, water- and vodka-liking algae specialists, animalistic zoologists, and butterfly specialists – aethereal, slim flibbertigibbets.

Fire

Fire is what makes us human. We used it before we even became *Homo sapiens,* when we were still some other kind of *Homo.* .... layers of ash in caves are proof of this.

Fire is as wild and unrestrained as a primitive warrior. At the same time, it was controlled by our wild ancestors – used to scare away predators and for hunting for ungulates or even for locusts. It warmed hairless monkeys, allowing them to travel this far north.

As a child, I loved burning grass. Field burning in spring has a lot to do with magic. One unassuming action – a match thrown into dry stalks – creates metres of flames and smoke that trails for miles.

Around Krosno, many beautiful grassy territories have retained their flora thanks to children setting them on fire in spring. Of course this eliminates some organisms, but it also provides space for many others.

I once gave an interview to a local radio station about the positive effects of burning grass. At that very moment my neighbour called to tell me that my forest was on fire! Another neighbour was burning grass and accidentally set the young birch and sycamore forest aflame. When I got there, the fire service had already put out the fire. It was then that I fully understood its dangerous power.

Fire gave a great advantage to the hominids that learned to maintain it. It provided protection from animals, the ability to use it for sculpting, and, most importantly, enabled them to prepare meals. Meat prepared in the fire was free of parasites and the high temperature allowed people to eat plants that are inedible or even very poisonous when eaten raw. Animals are scared of fire and so it could also be used to chase them away. A rarely appreciated benefit of fire is also the ability to carve vessels with the use of embers. The ability to burn extensive areas of forests and practice the so-called 'slash-and-burn' was also a great achievement. It's the way some tribes cultivate plants in the Amazon, Mexico, Laos or Indonesia to this day. A portion of the forest is cut down and burned once the cut plants have dried up. But in some places before the invention of farming people used fire for hunting, sometimes even picking up partly charred animals from the ashes. It's interesting that we humans are able to run a good few metres over hot coals without burning our feet. Maybe it's a form of evolutionary adaptation to the picking out of prey from conflagrations.

A trip to the Tatra Mountains

We 'civilised humans' are privileged in our access to a multitude of things. I don't even mean food or comfort, but for instance being able to get into a car and just drive off. We can get from one end of Europe to another in a day by getting on the motorway. The amount of different restrictions that concerned primitive humans was enormous. These limitations can be discovered even during a simple camping trip during which instead of having the central heating of our houses we need to satisfy ourselves with trying to stay warm by a fire made out of firewood we collected ourselves. But some things were easier – we didn't have to get up just to send our kids to school or go to work only in order to earn money for an exotic holiday or a better car than our neighbour's.

Certain limitations of life in the past become tangible when moving from the city to the countryside. We exchange concrete pavements for muddy paths, gas heating for wood we have to chop up ourselves, and the hundred metre ascent up to our houses in winter becomes a challenge.

When buying land to live on, I focused on size. I wanted to buy one single and large piece of land, as cheap as possible of course – I didn't have much money. It was difficult to come by a single large piece of land in the Polish mountains that I wanted to live in. Fields are scattered and barely any landowners could dream of a twelve acre plot of land, while cottages for sale usually had at most a garden to offer. Many stretches of fields for sale in the Lower Beskids after the dissolution of State Agricultural Farms (called PGRs) were really cheap (back then in 1996) but there were usually few trees on them. I fell in love with a piece of land in Pietrusza Wola in Pogórze Dynowskie, where forty-two acres of scenic hillsides were for sale thanks to the fact that six neighbouring landowners gave their land over to the government in exchange for benefits. So I bought it. The guy who measured the trees before making an auction estimate, said: 'Don't buy this Sir, there's no river here. I've got my eye on just a couple of acres but they're right next to the scenic Jasiołka river'. I ignored him back then but now I understand the importance of his words. Although I'm happy with my land, I now understand the value of a large river. The valley of a river is another world, different habitats, riverside thickets, fish, snails, water birds. And so during my survival workshops, we travel from my piece of land five miles to the river. Because everywhere is the same until you get to that point at which you can suddenly find different plants and animals. This is also why it was so important for humans to be within reach of a body of water. Only such a place would have been attractive and easy to find. The Machiguenga in Peru managed to keep to their primitive mixed agricultural-hunting economy thanks to the fact that they were far away from the river. My land was cheap for the same reason – it was inaccessible, far from the river. You can't have it all!

So we have a river. Of course it would be handy to be near a lake and the sea. There are so many useful species that can be found in places that lie at once by the sea, a lake, a stream, the woods... I think of Tallin, the capital city of Estonia.

Every variation in environment drew primitive people to itself like a magnet. There was no Internet or TV, no books, and their window on the world was the top of the hill. This is why people are drawn to friendly low hills (by the river of course!) more than to flatlands. Unless the flatland is adjacent to hills. This is the case for Kraków, Turin, Xi'an, Beijing, Sandomierz, Rzeszów, and Tarnów. We have a sandy plain in front of us and clay or limestone hills behind us. Different soil, different flowers, different trees, as well as the ability to look further forward into the distance. The bigger the hills, the more choice of plants and climate zones. We can move from the flat land where Xi'an

147

is located to mountain ranges of 4000 m above sea level within one day on horseback. From the heated persimmon, pomegranate, and jujube groves move first into a land of oaks, then birches and linden, then fir trees, and finally high-altitude thickets and meadows. Without a car, we can do this only in the mountains. In southern China or northern India it takes two days to walk from the subtropics to the alpine tundra. Such diversity was within a beggar's reach. What richness of experiences in comparison with the flatland swamps of Eastern Europe!

If I lived at the foot of the Tatras, I would collect birch and sycamore sap at the bottom, and then do this higher and higher up as spring went on, until the end of April. I could then collect acorns in the foothills 'at the bottom', beech nuts at the montane level and Swiss pine nuts at the subalpine level, and stuff myself with cooked carline thistles.

I think eastern Mexico contains one of the most varied biomes in the world. I'm in Xalapa, in the capital of the state of Veracruz, over a thousand metres above sea level. The warm, moist cloud forest rises beneath the city. I take a bus west. Within two hours, we drive through the main mountain range, passing meadows as well as beech and pine forests, just like in Europe. The bus slowly rolls downhill. It's dry on the other side of the mountains. There are *Opuntia* and other cacti. Rattlesnakes, scorpions and vultures. In the distance lies the highest peak of Mesoamerica – Pico de Orizaba. Heat pours out of the sky. I stop a coach after getting some tacos in some roadside booth in El Limon Totalco. It takes me to the coast. We drive downhill, passing Xalapa, and then both dry forests and savannahs. Veracruz is sandy, there are fish in the markets and mangrove forests nearby. All the biomes on Earth a couple hours on the bus away.

Dungeons

One of the most interesting cases of derivative rewilding I know is of a Russian World War One soldier who apparently spent eight years in the basement of Fort XIII in Bolestraszyce near Przemyśl. Trapped underground, he survived many years first eating tinned food, then rats. He got used to living in a constant temperature of just a few degrees. His hair and nails grew long and he came to hate light and noise. He died soon after being brought back to the surface.

This story might just be legend. Someone apparently admitted to fabricating it for the pre-war Polish press. I remember taking part in a shoot for my sister's film in the Łagiewniki Forest in Łódź. The scene involved a dead deer (bought in a hunting shop – I got to eat it later) and my daughter. It was a winter full of wet snow. I sat in the old Robur van and kept myself busy with making teas and coffees for the film crew. The driver seemed bored and munched on a salad, bragging about not eating bread because of his diet. I proposed he should try grasshoppers and told him that I eat them sometimes.

'That's nothing,' he said. 'You only eat them sometimes, but in the mountains there's this guy who eats only insects. I read an interview with him in *Gazeta Wyborcza*.'

Of course he was talking about me, but it's so easy to confuse *sometimes* with *always*.

149

Rousseau

When writing about the good savage, it is impossible not to mention Rousseau. Jean-Jacques Rousseau was a Swiss French-speaking writer and one of the most gifted creators of the Enlightenment. His tribute to natural harmonious wildness is probably the most famous in the history of literature. He was (in theory) an enemy of civilization. He negated the value of progress, money, paid work, and civilization in his pedagogical work: *Emile, or On Education* (1762). His books were highly acclaimed, and he became one of the most influential thinkers of his time. However, Rousseau is also one of the best examples of how theory can diverge from practice. His ideas were lofty, egalitarian, progressive, and anarchist in a good sense of the word. In practice, he sent a few of his children to an orphanage and spent his life supported by rich women.

Natural and wild

In this book, I use the adjectives *wild* and *natural* interchangeably. *The Dictionary of Contemporary Polish* defines the term *natural* as the following:

1. in accord with nature; organic, true, real;

2. part of someone's natural way of being; inbred, innate;

3. leaving no doubt; obvious, normal;

4. effortless, unforced, honest, common.

I will not provide a full definition for what is wild, because it would encompass a much more extensive list of synonyms. The meaning of *wild* is related not only to the *natural*, but also to *crazy, unbridled, brutal, maladjusted.*

I don't think that everything that is natural is also wild. A natural human will sometimes behave cruelly or indomitably, and at other times stay calm, relaxed, and passive.

Matriarchy and patriarchy

Indo-Europeans are patriarchal – we are used to inheriting our surnames from our fathers, are the authors of world wars, and warriors and rulers of the galaxy fascinate us – even though the past few decades have shifted the benefit towards women and their leading role in society (matriarchy). What was it like in the beginning? No-one knows. Of course, we can guess. I direct anyone interested to Zygmunt Krzak's work *Od matriarchatu do patriarchatu* [*From Matriarchy to Patriarchy*]. Krzak is a fan of matriarchy. He claims that it was present in most Paleolithic societies, it had its place at the very beginnings of humanity which only later began to move towards patriarchy.

However, not everyone agrees with him. I'm sure many anthropologists would say that in the beginning, there was a greater balance between the sexes. But it's still a fact that roles were divided. Currently there is only one hunter-gatherer tribe, the Agta in the Philippines, in which women hunt. The banal division into the woman mother and hunter and the male hunter is, in most cases, true. But even among a large number of patriarchal primitive hunting societies or hoe farmers, name inheritance occurs on the female line. It makes sense: the mother's always sure that her child is hers,

151

but it's not so obvious who its father is. From this perspective, our system of inheriting surnames is funny. Some people bear the surnames of the husbands of their mothers, who conceived with a neighbour or postman or pizza delivery guy (*pizza sex* is now a category on porn websites). Their surnames are useless labels.

We are also currently used to treating all of our ancestors equally – the mother of the father of our mother the same as the mother of the father of our father. In many cultures, one only belongs to the male or female line, and ancestors are only counted in a straight line – all that matters is the mother of the mother of our mother or the father of the father of our father. The latter pattern corresponds to the Biblical lists of the ancestors of Joseph from the house of David.

At first glance, it would appear that our ancestors are all equal. But that's not completely true. There are two lines that carry the most shared genetic information – on the female (distaff) and the male (spear) side of the family. Our DNA is mostly gathered in chromosomes in the nucleus. However, a separate strand of DNA is stored in the mitochondria – the cell organelles. The ancestors of those organelles were bacteria that lived in our cells millions of years ago. Mitochondria play an important part in the breathing process and certain genetic illnesses to do with cellular respiration, the symptoms of which can include issues with correct muscle function, may be encoded in them. But most importantly, we only inherit our mitochondria from our mothers. Sperm lives for too short a time to have any. Mitochondria are passed on only by the egg, and throughout history they have been altered only by quite rare mutations. By comparing two people, the number of differences in their mutations, we are able to say how many generations ago their family trees diverged. This is how the concept of a 'mitochondrial Eve' was born and how it was finally proven that our beginnings were in Africa.

Luckily for men, it is also possible to study purely male lines. The Y chromosome, responsible for the male sex, is passed on only by sperm. This way, we can compare the ancestry of people with the same surnames to check whether they all come from the same close ancestor. I was recently contacted by a woman from California with the same surname as mine. She paid for my genetic test to compare my Y chromosome with her brothers'. And what did we find out? The sequences were the same... Then it turned out that our families came from two neighbouring villages and that our family lines split ways in the XIX century.

Party

I'm standing in front of a big hall. There's a party inside. Lights flicker to the thud of techno. Girls on acid and ecstasy bend rhythmically to the music.

I had an anthropologist friend who, whenever I would take out a CD with contemporary music, would make a face as if forced to drink a glass of vinegar. 'It's not for me' – he'd say – 'culture's fallen, traditions have faded away, this is rubbish'.

But these people reminded me of tribal dance. And it's interesting that they didn't make him think of the same. What mattered to him was the message. Whatever had an unclear, broken message, didn't count, which was pretty incoherent – he himself was interested in shamans, who received messages from ghosts, not fathers…

Again we arrive at the conflict between tradition and revelation, between the Pharisees, who represented tradition, and Jesus, who was preaching something new. 'You will know them by their fruits' – I reminded my anthropologist. You'll also recognise the party by its fruits.

Long, long ago, religious beliefs used to change much faster than in modern-day churches. Maybe even as fast as the Internet. People were in direct contact with spirits and prophetic dreams modified their behaviour. Here, it's worth mentioning Peter Nabokov's book *Two Leggings: the making of a Crow warrior*. It's the largely autobiographical story of the development of one person, a tale of a Plains Indian in search for trips and dreams. This book shows the great lability of tradition. Most Plains Indians conduct the sweat lodge ritual in a small wigwam with one entrance from the East. However, the character has a vision that the tribe should be cleansed by entering the wigwam through two entrances – from the East and from the West. Contrary to tradition. It's dangerous, but the elders allow him to perform the ritual to measure the force of Two Leggings' dreams. The rite is successful (I think it had something to do with hunting for bison). The dreams' force is confirmed. Techno-party participants, let me know whether your visions after taking LSD had force? Fruits tell us everything. The DNA of our children are our basic fruits. Our visions have been preformulated so that their fruit is the flourishing of our tribe, children, children, children. The only fruitful parties are those which result (sometimes in the long run) in some form of conception.

Cross-breeding with chimpanzees

To prove our obvious proximity to apes to the sceptic, we would need to experiment by cross-breeding a human with a chimpanzee. It's not so obvious because our genomes have a few different chromosomes. I don't tell my students about this, but ask them a serious question: 'Which of you (for, I assume, a large sum of money) would be willing to cross-breed with a chimp?' The answer took me aback. One third of the women in the classroom raised their hands (they were studying teaching of foreign languages). None of the men did. The women don't see a large difference between a man and a chimp. The bell rang and I didn't manage to establish to what extent the answer was about money.

Natural numbers

Natural numbers come from God. The devil invented fractions. Primitive hunter-gatherers weren't mathematical experts. Scientists have found tribes that count only up to three, four, or five. The results of research on the Pirahã language still came as a real shock. The Pirahã tribe lives in the basin of the Amazon river, in Brazil. Their language has fascinated linguists for decades and no-one could understand it. The Pirahã didn't know any other languages, so it was impossible to translate their language. This was finally achieved by the anthropologist and linguist Daniel Everett, who devoted most of his life to studying this group of people. He arrived there with his family as a protestant missionary, but, in the meantime, was converted, or rather inverted, by the tribe – for they don't have a clear system of beliefs. The Pirahã don't believe in ghosts. Sometimes they see them. If they can't see them, they stop believing in them. Their language not only lacks numerals, but also words for colours, numbers, genders, or tenses. Their society cannot remember events further back than two generations. They speak only about what is within the range of the present, and, more rarely, in the near past. They are settled in the concrete. Why use numbers? After all, Katie and Andrew aren't the same as Katie and Anne. Everything makes a difference.

I hate this country

When coming back from a shopping trip in the nearby town of Krosno, especially on a grey winter day, I usually think: 'I hate this country, I hate these people'. Sarah and I talked so many times about moving to another country (she actually left for Scotland six years later...). Our fingers trace their way round the map of the world. England? Morocco? Thailand? India? America? We both hate the dumb faces of the shopkeepers in Krosno shops, their perpetual sourness, fear of conversation, and reluctance to interact with us.

Although most hunter-gatherers were nomads, they didn't usually wander at random – they usually circled around their territory, visiting spots for hunting and plant collection, depending on the season. The Australian Aborigines believed that they do not own land, but that the land owns them, so there was no way they could leave the land where their ancestors lie, where the spirits guard them.

Meanwhile, very many contemporary seekers of neo-wildness escape the places they come from. Young, nature-loving people usually run away from countries of the North which are swept by cold winds: the Netherlands, Germany, Great Britain. They move to the Mediterranean or further, somewhere into the tropics. Others, despite difficult conditions, do prefer the North, where there are places full of empty wilderness, like Alaska, which drew the protagonist of 'Into the Wild'.

I chose to stay put. After a few years of living in Warsaw, I returned to my Carpathian home. I moved away twelve kilometres away from where I spent my childhood. That distance can be walked in two hours... I moved to hills which were a myth to me as a child. On the horizon, these hills overgrown with forest seemed unattainable. One could say I haven't got very far in life.

Yet still I hesitate. I hate winter. I can't say I love hot weather, but every temperature below ten degrees Celsius seems inhuman. I would happily escape to some subtropical hills with a fresh but warm climate. I once took a Facebook quiz called 'Which nationality are you?'. I got Berber.

But the ghosts stop me. I remain bound by the eternal umbilical cord of birth, caught in the net of beings who existed near the place I now live in. It's a natural conservativeness.

When I was twenty-three years old, I nearly began a PhD in Oklahoma. Then one day I had a dream. It was March. Burned grass, I'm climbing a hill near Krosno, I dig a hole at the top. A golden chalice shines inside. It's half a metre tall. When I woke up in the morning, I cancelled my travel plans and that afternoon, I got a letter informing that I received a scholarship from the Foundation for Polish

Science. Ten thousand Polish zlotys, which covered nearly half of the price of the land I now live on.

But I'm still waiting for the moment my ancestors' spirits tell me: 'You can go'. I'll then dig up the bones of my grandparents from the cemetery in Krosno, polish them, wrap them in my great-gran's canvas bag and walk straight ahead into the Atlas Mountains. 'Inshallah.

Loneliness and community

Seekers of wildness are often solitary daredevils, oddballs, madmen, mystics; sometimes couples, rarely communities. Meanwhile, primitive people lived in a group, a tribe. In many tribes, going to the jungle alone is considered deadly dangerous. Not only because of snakes, but of spirits.

Life in a primitive community consisted not only in the neighbourhood of bodies and actions – it involved a different way of perceiving the scope of human freedom and ego. In primitive societies, the individual was entirely assigned to their community and assigned to the land of their ancestors. Humans do not exist in isolation. The group's rejection is the largest possible punishment, comparable to a death sentence.

The Papuans

New Guinea is subject to common Western mistaken stereotypes. It is associated with wild people hidden deep in the jungle, their septa pierced with bones, who eat their relatives. It's true that cannibalism did (or perhaps still does) occasionally take place there. Still, New Guinea is a country of farmers. The tribes of New Guinea mostly cultivate different local edible plants, sometimes even building large irrigation ditches in their fields, and breed pigs. Their famed liking for cannibalism may be caused by scarceness of meat (most of their food consists of starchy plants). Hence the amount of insects eaten in New Guinea. The case is similar in Thailand, where for poor inhabitants of the Isaan province who eat mainly rice, grasshoppers, stink bugs, or cicadas are not a fancy dish, but above all a source of protein and precious fatty acids.

Bison

The bison is the king of the Primeval Forest. Not only the Białowieża Forest. He's also king in the village Wysoka Strzyżowska, a village two miles from my house. I'm sitting here in Cameroon bar drinking my bison beer from Dojlidy brewery with a foreman named Arm. This company puts pictures of wild animals on their beer cans.

'You, Władek, tell me why guys these days drink all that bison stuff?'

'Cause it's cool to look at,' Arm replied wisely, waving his finger.

Trance

One could spend a long time arguing about how to define trance. Trance is a bag into which we throw states of mind that differ from daily states – states in which we are at least partly unable to react to stimuli from our environment. Even watching television can be a trance.

When healing and prophesizing, tribal shamans would often fall to the ground in convulsions, with foam at the mouth, sometimes insensitive to pain to the point that they could be stabbed with sharp tools. Only in such a state of mind were they able to act effectively.

Reality, however, is distracting. A change in our state of mind allows for an alternative view of the stimuli that reach us. On one hand, it allows us to notice trivial stimuli which are unobservable in normal awareness – this happens, for instance, when we take mushrooms or LSD. On the other hand, it focuses our psychic energy and power. Our daily ways of life, richness in stimuli, short-term activities interrupted by others, and abundance of food make it difficult to enter a trance. Trance is achieved either by using plants or magic mushrooms, or by dancing for many hours, or by starving or not sleeping for many days, or by listening to rhythmical monotonous music, OR all of these at the same time.

Theta rhythms (4-7 Hz) are especially conducive to 'trance' states, autosuggestion, and clairvoyance. They correspond to the frequencies our brains display before sleep. They mark the verge of sleep and waking life.

The power of rhythmic music was known not only to primitive tribes. Since the XVI century, the European infantry has also known the power of marching to the rhythm of a drum. Monotonous prayers, rosaries, and litanies stimulate similar states.

Sugar

Diabetes is a XXI century disease, a result of always having full plate. With the exception of a small percentage of diabetics in whom something 'went wrong', most 'earned' it. People who don't eat enough, who walk, fast, hunt, and eat the meat of wild animals roasted in parcels of leaves, don't get diabetes. It's the price we pay for chips, lemonade, and chocolate, for cars and a sofa with a TV. We are a civilization of sugar.

We spent centuries desperately trying to fill our stomachs and struggling with famine. Primitive hunter-gatherers were also often full. But not always. Sometimes they starved. They ate lean meat, fibrous bulbs, nuts, and sometimes honey. Their times were marked with low sugar levels in blood, which was conducive to trance, visions, hallucinations. A holistic way of viewing the world, contact with spirits. With lowered levels of sugar in blood, on the verge of the norm, we are unable to think – to think like a scientist, I.T. specialist or accountant – but our muscles still work, we can keep singing, talking, walking, and having emotions and visions. When our sugar levels rise a little, when we are not hungry, we become less jittery and more inclined to think, plan, plot, devise intrigues. That's what the twentieth century was like. And what about the twenty-first? Will it be a century of such sugar levels that we will all fall into a diabetic coma?

Wild honey

As I mentioned in a different section, most tropical primitive tribes know of and love honey. Sometimes they even cut down trees that are a hundred metres tall in order to reach a single wild hive. For a long time, I dreamed of finding wild bees in the forest, but our climate is harsh and they're hard to come by. The bees came themselves. They started a nest in the wall of my neighbour's house, in its mineral wool. Their great kingdom filled the entire top of my neighbour's hut. One day, I thought he had gone mad. He had taken apart the whole clapboard. As I came closer, I noticed there were a dozen of buckets next to him, with honeycomb in each.

'Shall we have a wild feast?' he said.

The honeycomb was delicious. Wax and honey, honey and wax, should not be separated. They taste best together. We got real wild bees from mineral wool.

I was lucky enough to try real jungle honey in Laos, ten years after starting to write the Polish version of this book. Lao markets are full of jungle food and bushmeat. It is actually very sad to look at monitor lizards with their feet tied with wire, pieces of python meat or women serially breaking legs of the frogs and toads they sell. But the mass of wild fruits, vegetables, mushrooms and insects brings paradise to mind. While writing the English version of this book I am making an inventory of wild foods sold in the markets of Luangprabang, the old capital of Laos. I have been to the morning market here over 40 times, in different seasons – during the dry one, at the beginning of the monsoon, in the middle of the monsoon and at the turn of the monsoon and the dry season. On most mornings I start my pageant around the market with buying wild bee brood baked on embers wrapped in banana leaves. Then I buy a small piece of a honeycomb from the jungle. Then in spring, when they are available, I get a handful of *kaimot*, ant 'eggs' (technically ant larvae). When I leave the market I go for a coffee. I order a double espresso and I throw the eggs into it. It nearly tastes like a latte…

Dziwożona

The 'dziwożona' is a combination of the words 'dziwa' and 'żona', which together originally meant 'wild woman'. In some Slavic languages to this day 'diva' is the female form of the adjective 'wild'. Our people also believed in them in places, and they went by different names. They would kidnap new-born children, swap them and leave their ugly ones behind. They had long breasts that sagged down to the ground. They lived in the woods. Women giving birth had to cover their child with St. John's wort in order to protect themselves.

The dziwożonas and their special plant, the common polypody, were popularised by the writer Seweryn Goszczyński (1803-1876). They are characters in his poems *Sobótka* and *Dziennik podróży do Tatrów*. Dziwożonas also have red hats with common polypody in them. This fern has sweet rhizomes which were eaten by children and shepherds in some areas. In XIX-century town of Jasło in southeastern Poland they were even sold in the market. In *Sobótka*, Goszczyński included the following song that illustrates the initiation for a dziwożona:

Włosy ci rozplotą,

163

Czapeczkę nasadzą,
Słodyczkę jeść dadzą

[They will undo your plait,
Adorn you with a hat,
And give you the polypody fern to eat]

It is really interesting that *diva*, wild, has also connection with the Sanskrit *diva* and Roman *deus*, meaning god or supernatural being. Thus the Slavic *div, divy, diva* and the like started as 'godly', 'spirited'! In Indo-European languages there seemed to be three categories of supernatural beings with names starting from the letters D, B and G. Compare three names of God: Latin – *deus*, English – *god*, and Polish – *bóg*. And now look at Polish *gad* – meaning 'reptile', 'monster' and English *bug* – meaning some small insect-like, or disliked creature. Thus we see a triangle of three concepts – a good god, a bad, nasty monster and something wild transforming from one to another, when changing the language!

The answer

Is there an answer to the question of whether it is possible to become a wild human again? Yes and no. A total return to a hunter-gatherer lifestyle, without any of civilization's achievements, is possible in an at least moderately warm place for a short period of time: a few weeks or at most a few years. It's an extreme choice, one in which we wouldn't stand a chance of bringing up children. It's a choice for the desperate and lonely or for groups of hermits. Of course the more elements of civilization we keep, the greater our chance of success. Even the small things count: canvas for our shelter, a bottle for water, the top of a can to be made into a knife, a bottle of oil, a kilogram of flour, and at best a credit card on a string, a suburban rubbish bin or a family that can shelter us in the winter.

Evolution

The nineteenth-century fathers of anthropology – the so-called evolutionists – claimed that societies evolve from 'wildness' – that is, primitive hunter-gatherers, through 'barbarism' to civilization. This thesis was then usually contested by their successors but it's currently being often returned to. Neo-revolutionists show the importance for different cultures of how much food they can produce and what methods they use. Hunter-gatherers were able to feed very few people out of a single square kilometre. The effectiveness of use (exploitation!) of the land grew with the perfection of farming methods. Along with the development of farming, a smaller and smaller amount of increasingly perfected species of land animals, water animals and plants have been eaten until we have arrived at a stage at which most of the population of the earth eats a few species of grains, vegetables, and animals, except for some rich individuals from the top of this pyramid and surviving wild tribes. Thanks to the lowered costs of food we do, however, have more freedom in other spheres – we can move around, choose our careers, and claim ownership over many things.

Those who want to return to a life as hunter-gatherers should not advertise it. If even a quarter of their compatriots listened to them, they would empty the country of all edible animals and most edible plants within a year and still go hungry. In our times of climate crisis and global overpopulation, trying too hard to be hunter-gatherers seems quite selfish and wrong.

In that case, is it still worth trying? Yes, but with full awareness of the possibility of failure and the chance of... partial success. There are many unused niches in nature. A partial return to a hunter-gatherer lifestyle is, then, advisable, as long as it does not lower the incredibly valuable coexistence of a few billion people with the many millions of species of organisms on Earth that we have managed to preserve so far. So let's go mushroom picking in the woods, or fishing from time to time, and collect nettles for our soups. Let's look through our local rubbish dumps and eat untouched chips left behind in bars, but not leave traps for bison or throw stones at birds.

A seasonal return to a Paleolithic lifestyle can be treated as a new kind of ritual of getting back in touch with nature. There's no point in suddenly abandoning all products of civilization – we would eat each other alive. It is, however, important to keep each tiny element of our Paleolithic customs. For the good of our psyches and bodies. We've not been civilised people for long.

I think the school system is the furthest behind. At school, children spend a few hours a day being force-fed unnatural numbers and unnatural information.

Instead, teachers should take children to the forest, for a month, to shelters they have built themselves. Children should bathe from time to time in a cold pond and be told to dig out wild bulbs. Chocolate bars and Coca-Cola should be thrown out of school shops. Each school should be supplied with a barrel of sauerkraut and a loaf of sourdough bread, smoked fish and a block of cheese.

Children should be able to identify all of the flowers in their forest. And during the Holy Week, they should fast for a couple of days in a special camp in the middle of the woods.

Wildness should be a pyramid – with what is healthy common to all people at its base, and what is strange, rare, difficult, but still required by the recesses of the soul at its top.

St. John's Eve

Tomasz lived in a block of flats in Krosno, but he loved mountains, the forest, streams, and wandering around. He spent every weekend outdoors with his wife. They both worked in an office, so they were drawn to the country. They ordered a Native American tipi from their friend, and set it up outside a village, by the forest, on their private meadow they had recently purchased. Every other weekend, instead of hiking, they would spend Friday and Saturday night in it. They also invited their friends round. They managed to assemble a whole crowd of nature-lovers. Together, they went fishing, picked mushrooms, and practiced tree climbing.

His wife went on a last minute holiday to Croatia with her friend. That Saturday, he sat alone in his tent. It was meant to be St. John's Eve. He made a small fire and looked into the flames. With his mind's eye, he could see the pre-

Slavic orgies that took place on that day. Wild shrieks, couples copulating somewhere in the bushes. So how did they do it, did they go off in pairs or all make out in the same square? This will remain a mystery, but he himself would probably prefer the square.

With his mind's eye, he could see a group of his friends celebrating. They would probably be impossible to convince. But maybe? Different versions of the orgy kept coming into mind. But he was a very practical and careful person. What about AIDS and pregnancies? There are always condoms, but he hated them. Maybe it would be better to masturbate around the fire? Or tie the women to trees? He couldn't imagine being tied up – he wouldn't be able to manage it. He was fidgety and people said he had ADHD. Should he buy a pack of latex gloves and change them as he massages each pussy? What about animal masks? He once saw a film about an orgy in masks. But he only had the masks of carol singers: the Shepherd, Herod, and the *turoń* (bull) – a horned festive animal. Most likely all of the girls would want to get off with the bull... Maybe it would be better to use some natural massaging materials? Yew berries, large slugs? Maybe both, or maybe he ought to submerge the latex gloves in a mush of forest fruits? Perhaps they should whip their genitalia with birch branches? Roll around in mud? In ash? The escalation of his ideas and imaginings would have probably made him come if not for a rustling outside. Radek, a neighbouring villager, entered the shelter.

'Could you lend me twenny zlotys?' he says.

'What for?' asks Tomasz.

'We're making a bonfire for summer solstice.'

'I'll pay today' Tomasz said with pride.

They went to the local shop. Tomek bought twenty beers (hoping it'll be enough?) and a bag of sausages.

'Now that's what I call a party' said Radek. 'Alcohol, sausages and girls, not some return to nature, he, he.'

Tomek started making the fire while Radek went to get the 'team'. Two guys and three girls turned up. He knew all of them. After a few beers, the party began to get going and the conversation became engaging (at first he felt like they had nothing to talk about).

Radek asked: 'And you, do you fuck at those Indian meetups of yours?'

'Not really, I guess everyone feels like it but it somehow never works out that way' Tomek replied.

'So what do you do, like, drink?' Radek asked.

'Not really, we want to return to nature.'

'That's the whole problem. We have a crate of beer and a fire, so it's easy. We don't need any returning to nature, nature comes to us itself.' Radek answered. 'You'll see today', he added with a whisper. I will fuck them all.

Electricity

The extent to which electricity has changed human life can be seen whenever the cables are brought down by a storm. Disorganisation occurs on two levels. On an organisational level, we can't use our computers, food starts to melt in our freezers, and so on. Then there's the level of perception of the world. We are used to strong lighting all the way into the night. Suddenly, evenings lengthen, we have to spend hours in the dark lit up by candles or fire from the fireplace. Lack of light makes us aware of the dark, the evening creeping up. We become more sensitive to sound, tolerant towards dirt and less concerned with the crumbs we spilled on the floor. We fall asleep early, and in the morning the sun greets us like a true deity. We use every hour, like a pauper sucking on the last crumb of bread.

I recently got hold of a book called *How to live without electricity* which tells about the life of the Amish, a protestant group of Christians who negate progress. They have stopped at the level of development their world was in when they were first formed. Their church was first formed by a small group of two hundred settlers who arrived in the USA in the XVIII century. There are currently a few thousand of them. They have retained a dialect of German. They are very conservative in their reception of technological achievements. In many aspects, they seem to be frozen in time, stuck in the XVIII century, although some communities have decided to accept certain developments, for instance phone boxes. They have no electricity or other conveniences which would make them dependent on the outside world.

The Amish are living proof of how little humans need to function happily. They farm fairly effectively without the use of modern farming equipment. They have horse carriages and don't use phones in their houses, believing that such inventions impede normal meetings in the neighbourhood.

The Amish also refuse to pay social insurances, send kids above the age of fourteen to school (they have their own schools), vaccinate, or complete army service. For these reasons, they have had numerous feuds with state authorities, but they usually win! Maybe a community of a few thousand people already has its voice. The constancy

170

and vitality of their beliefs, as well as the low percentage of leavers (around twenty percent), is truly astonishing.

Ass

Wieśka lives on the edge of the village. She's eighty, but she looks like she's sixty. She's a childless widow. Her cottage is neat, she has a pretty garden, a few goats, and an old orchard. Quite an idyllic landscape. She's a simple but wise and insightful woman. She also knows a lot about herbs. The cottage is filled with smoke and dirt by 'European standards' but she airs it out pretty often. Wieśka is dressed in some rags. Her house smells of apple compote, walnuts she has put away in boxes, and mice.

When I ask her if she minds the mice, she says: 'No, but I mind the rats, cause they bite'. Another time, she says 'I once had some mice drown in me sauerkraut. Twas dark but I cooked em up. They were good but crunchy.'

She doesn't light the fire much. Sometimes she brings some branches from the forest, always huddled up in those rags. She probably sleeps in them, too.

She fascinates me as a symbol of harmony. Maybe I'll be the same when I grow old?

Searching for wisdom in her, some Mediterranean or Caucasian miracle diet for hundred-year-olds, I ask her what she eats: 'Bread n butter, bread n lard, bread n pâté. Whatever I have. I'm not fussy.' 'What makes a healthy life?' I ask.

'You gotta pray and move yer ass a bit. If I didn't work in the fields n chop my wood n got on those buses I'd be in the grave by now. You gotta move yer ass, that's the important thing. Weed the potatoes, or with a man, or go up the hill to that other shop where the bread's cheaper, or go round the church in circles thirty times. The ass has gotta keep movin'.'

The mountain didn't come to Mohammad, Mohammad came to the mountain

Wojciech Jankowski's *Dumki Jacoba* (Jacob's Thoughts) is a short and sweet book that inspired me to write this book. It also suggested its form to me. Short contemplative pieces on different subjects, including returning to nature, as Jacob also used to live in the Carpathians like me. I also got my hands on it on a book-shelf shelf visiting my friends. I feel like the continuator of that book. 'Dumki' are a diminutive term for thoughts. I could call mine *Dumki Łukasza* (*Łukasz's Thoughts*).

I spent a few years collecting myself to order this book and kept forgetting. Then one day I got a letter from Jacob himself – he sent me a signed copy! So he thought of me when he heard about my activities and workshops. How nice.

Contamination

I was at my friends' house. I was eating crisps which I normally don't do, but it was New Year's Eve and I'd already had two beers. Then damn, they were gone. I crumpled up the packet and instinctively threw it into the fire. My host shouted: 'Łukasz, I didn't expect this from you.'

I explained that I did this through inattention, but she was still sour. It had contaminated her stove. Maybe it was the first time something so disgusting had found its way in there. A plastic packet that dioxins and other carcinogenic stuff will leap out of like demons. And I guess she was right. Most of us are unaware how harmful it is to burn plastic, at least here, in the countryside.

And then I began to wonder if the same goes for wildness as for contamination avoidance or critical mass. Let's take contamination. Let's assume there exists a primitive, idyllic state of wildness in which we could find a Hunter-Gatherer in a Primeval Forest. It's enough to show him some beads or a camera, or give him a plastic bottle, and he will stop being a primitive human. We can also contaminate – 'deprimevalise' – the Primeval Forest by making a narrow path right through its middle, cutting out one tree, or killing all the bison.

And now the concept of critical mass. Let's say that in order to become a wild human, you have to collect a certain amount of points. After crossing some threshold, we are Wild.

One point for mushroom picking, fishing, and walks in the woods.

For life in a shelter in the forest all year round – 365 points. One for each day.

For collecting wild plants – also some points.

And some for hunting deer, for eating snails and insects.

Of course it depends on what weapons we are using. If a shotgun, multiply by ½. Points for no gun at all.

20 points for animistic beliefs.

For every wife or husband above one – 100 points.

Points for attaining a trance state at least once a year.

Points for penile subincision, scarification, etc.

Points for calories consumed without the use of money.

For walking naked – also a point or two.

For dumpster diving in some suburban bin – one point.

For eating hedgehogs and run-over cats – some more points.

And so on and so forth. If we reach 1000 points a year, we are a New Wild Human. The idol of scouts and some anthropologists. And it doesn't matter that we decided to be wild humans only for eleven months and take a monthly holiday back to civilization for a month each year once we become a professor of anthropology who will be able to talk about those 11 months. We could even start recruiting students to join the tribe and become lecturers of anthropology, pedagogy, sociology, the psychology of wildness. How about a *wildness science*?

Cat

Bolek already had a house in the country, but then he inherited another one from his gran close by. As he was feeling a little lonely, he wanted someone interesting to live in it. He allowed a couple of friends to spend the winter there. Hania and Paweł were freaks. They didn't have stable jobs but saved some money every year from working in Norway. They were easy to get along with, they took care

174

of the cottage, cleaned and painted it. All good, except for the cat.

Bolek hated animals. He, a lover of nature, who cultivated all sorts of fantastic plants in his garden, who loved nettles in his soup, and the moose that looked through his window. But he couldn't understand why people keep pets.

Hania was vegetarian and even had a cat allergy. But as soon as they moved, someone pushed her into taking care of a cat. She bought it black pudding once a week but the cat was picky and meowed frightfully, demanding its favourite mackerel. It killed mice but didn't eat them.

A year passed. Hania and Paweł went back to Norway. Then they went on a trip to India.

'What about the cat?' Bolek asked.

'We'll leave him with you, he'll eat mice, and you can give him some of your leftovers from time to time.'

'But I hate cats.'

'Don't say that, you love nature.'

'But I'll kill it and eat it.'

'Oh come on, follow love vibrations, give it freedom.'

Hania gave Bolek a goodbye hug and added:

'It'll cope.'

But Bolek kept his word. He sharpened his Chinese cleaver he bought at a Vietnamese stool in Warsaw, grabbed the cat by its neck, stroked it and it purred with pleasure. Then suddenly it bellowed, blood shot out onto the wall, the cat started thrashing about in spasms of pain, causing the executioner to cut himself a little. The cut turned out to be very precise. Having lost its blood in extreme convulsions, the cat stopped moving.

Bolek gutted the cat in the same way you would gut a rabbit. He froze the head whole in a separate bag in the freezer. He made a goulash out of the rest. There was quite a lot of it. He ate it for two days seasoned with onion and carrot. He got quite fed up of it, so he added some sauerkraut, mushrooms, and prunes. Hunter's stew. Experimentally (and also in part to get rid of the cat stink) he added some prawn paste and soy sauce.

He leaned over his first bowl of this sort-of-hunter's-stew. Hania knocked on the door.

'Bolek, I forgot to return this book. What's that great smell?'

'A stew.'

'Too bad I'm veggie.'

'Nah, don't worry, it's just a kind of shrimp paste.'

'All right, I'll give it a try.'

Bolek prepared her a bowl, trying not to throw in any chunks of cat.

'Delicious. What about this piece? Is that fish?'

'No, it's your cat.'

From that day onwards, he carried a deep scar from Hania's teeth on his arm.

Dynamic Landscape

I'm currently reading a great monograph called *Dynamic Landscape*, edited by Nigel Dunnett and James Hitchmough. They specialise in the same thing as me – the verge of ecology and garden design. They create and study landscapes in English towns that imitate wild ones. While reading their book, it occurred to me that we can think of

176

the human search for nature analogously to the way we try to recreate wild landscapes in cities, in places where they have been destroyed.

The authors describe a whole spectrum of gardening activities which make a move towards the natural. So, first of all, they recreate environments. For example, we can start a forest in our garden that is meant to be a faithful copy of a forest of the kind that grows on the same soils in the area. We make a list of species, move plant cuttings from the neighbouring forest, collect seeds, and even introduce the right microorganisms and mushrooms by moving parts of the soil. How would this work with people? We would have to, for instance, find a few volunteers – the descendants of some until-recently-wild tribe, train them in survival skills, pass on knowledge gathered by ethnographers and place them in exactly the same environment and country in which their ancestors lived. A sort of similar experiment (but by no means a return to nature!) was made by the creation of Israel.

There are other ways in which we can naturalise landscape. We can select only native species without worrying too much about replicating the entire ecosystem, but only its basic functions. We could do something similar here – instead of making sure whether this tribe behaves exactly in the way it ought to, we would just let out the right people in the right place. Maybe they'll survive.

We also have the option to plant all sorts of non-native beautiful and fairly 'natural-looking' species of trees, bushes, and flowers and allow them to grow in a natural way, wildly, uncontrollably. A human equivalent of this would be to select a group of volunteers – survivalists, hippies, humans.

The fourth option is to plant native plants, but not in a chaotic, wild, or natural way, but in an urban manner – in alleyways, flowerbeds, strips in between roads. This would correspond to giving a living space to the last hunter-gatherers in our civilization, some sort of hunting rights, for example allowing them to hunt pigeons on the Main Square in Kraków.

Tribe

In 2006, Sarah put a newspaper down on the table.
'Here's something for you,' she said.
The article was about two British people, Bene Keene and Mark James, who created not a forum or support group but an internet tribe. They rented an island in Oceania, on Fiji from some tribe. The island could be accessed for a fee. Of course everything could be regulated by credit card by logging in on the site www.tribewanted.com. I then watched a documentary from this island. It showed the development of works on various buildings. No, let's not be naïve, the building work wasn't done by the Tribe of the Whites, but members of the Polynesian tribe.

The Hunter

I'm slowly reaching the end of my book. I'm tweaking words and paragraphs with the laptop on my knees and birch logs crackling in the fire. Some knocks on the door. Marek from the village from over the hill comes inside.

'Will you have a drink to celebrate my name day?' he asks.

'Okay, come in.'

I don't like sudden drunkenness but I guess I like him. I know he doesn't overdo it, we'll have a glass and he'll go to bed. But he was already really drunk, which I noticed once he sat down. He lay a gun down on the table.

'Are we drinking out of this?'

'No' – he took a bottle out of his pockets – 'but I carry it with me sometimes, you know, winter, hares, pheasants.'

And again I remembered about modern hunters.

'There's always gonna be meat for you,' I suggested.

'It's shit, not meat. you don't even get a kilogram out of a pheasant. But what sa-tis-fac-tion' he murmured. 'You know, pow, pow, blood, and you know straight away you're not just a piece of shit.' He roared with laughter here. 'Didn't you know I am the Great Hunter, the Great, the Greatest, I'll shoot all the deer' he roared and fell to the ground, a victim of Ukrainian Blagoff vodka and his own greatness.

Wild Life

I like the world wild and that's why I named my garden, my project: *the Wild Garden*. It's probably also natural that I read *Wild Life [Dzikie Życie]* – the periodical of Pracownia na Rzecz Wszystkich Istot [*Laboratory for All Beings*], an organisation devoted to the protection of the last remaining wild ecosystems in Poland. I always felt

179

ideologically close to them rather than those who only protect traditions to do with eating carp at Christmas.

I open the new issue of *Wild Life* and notice a motto that could well have served as the motto for this book. It is about the fact that when a culture cuts itself off from the wild side of life it automatically sentences itself to death. These words were written by Gary Snyder.

Gary Snyder is a great American writer and artist, a representative of the generation of the 60s and 70s, who was involved with the so-called *back-to-the-land-movement*.

Despite the fact that along with the development of material culture the importance of the city and large groups of people keeps growing, an opposing tendency towards returning to nature and quiet country life is still present, especially in times of crisis. Such a return was already praised by ancient poetry. It saved the lives of many people during the Great Depression in the 1930s in the USA or during the Nazi occupation in Poland. *The back-to-the-land-movement* happened during a time of American counter-culture, hippies, and contestation of the American notion of progress. Many intellectuals, activists, and those in search of a better world moved to the countryside. Land was still very cheap back then. As usual in the case of such movements, it turned out after a few years that a large proportion of people went back to the city. Those who remained were capable of combining the opportunities created by their environments by farming while writing or practicing a specialised craft on the side.

Millions are rotting here

Millions are rotting here! – a tour guide shouts to Western tourists in awe of the wilderness of the Białowieża Forest. They are riding in a carriage through the forest covered with felled trees. Rotting logs are home to many species of fungi and insects but they can also be made into planks (that's definitely what my neighbour would have done). In order to maintain the proliferation of our species, we have to keep ourselves alive. Most trees have to be made into planks and used as firewood and the land must be cultivated. However, temples to wilderness are necessary and we need to go back to them. The problem of modern man is not his dream of going back to complete wilderness. No, he dreams of having at least an inkling of wilderness and environmental conditions he was made for – clean water and air, a forest to walk in, a month off work spent in a tent, time to tell the kids stories and time for fishing.

What if some despot, the leader of some supranational government or of an American-Chinese-Russian coalition suddenly announced that farming and breeding are forbidden? We would be able to eat supplies of grains and slaughtered animals, then comb the surrounding forests for most edible bulbs. But there would be too many of us to satisfy our appetites. There's only about two acres of land per head in Poland. There's fifty times too many people for us to be able to sustain ourselves on the forest. We would stuff our stomachs with the leaves of nettles, linden trees, with thistles and other plants (the Irish trained themselves in this in the nineteenth century, the Chinese did so half a century ago, and North Koreans did this recently). However, our digestive systems are not created for eating only leaves. Our bulging stomachs would be filled with a green mass we would not be able to make full use of. Our shit would be green. Chętnik wrote about the XIX century famines in the region of Kurpie in Poland, during which people would wake up hungry, spend the whole day picking and eating nettles, and went to sleep still hungry. People would start to eat each other alive. Our civilization would break down, our blocks of flats would turn into jungle like the temple of Angkor Wat in Cambodia. Like the Mayan pyramids. Or it would become covered in elderflower and willow trees like the ruins of Warsaw after the war. And once the amount of people decreased, some rebels would return to cultivating land unless people could find some good way to regulate the population so that there were just enough of us to sustain ourselves on bulbs and deer. Although there would probably always end up being some idiots who want ten children and those children would then be forced to build civilization back in order to survive.

Pan

Everyone who wants to return to nature should pray to the Greek God Pan. He is portrayed with hairy goat legs, goat horns, and often with an erect penis. He is the companion of nymphs and symbolises vitality, spring, life, and sexuality. His name derives from the word for field. Pan brings together much of what modern civilization has disowned but which lies in human nature.

I wonder whether hairy-legged Pan excites or repels women who so obsessively shave not only their legs or armpits, but even the slightest trace of pubic hair. A wild human is a 'slightly-hairy' human. On the other hand, humans have battled with their body hair since prehistoric times. Native Americans relish in removing remains of their sparse body hair and archaeological sources stress that we were already inventing all sorts of haircuts thousands of years ago.

Pan is often associated with the orgiastic. Upon hearing the terms 'wild' or 'natural', a whole Pandora's box of visions of naked savages copulating in a fairly random way, like the chimps are accustomed to, springs to people's minds (I tested this in questionnaires for my students). But as I mentioned before, the sexuality of our wild ancestors may have been pretty straightforward. Large sexual freedom or orgies are usually limited to certain specific conditions – some large celebration, mourning, or great plenitude of food. Sexual freedom itself, which is related to the risk of unwanted pregnancy and even more unwanted diseases, is something very different to a strongly culturally relative fancifulness. In some cultures, displaying genitalia in public is something completely normal while in others it is completely shocking. It does not in itself carry any biological risks.

I think that while of course we may be biologically wired for small-scale polygamy, we are not specially biologically wired for orgies, which usually remain in the sphere of erotic phantasies, accusations, or experiences available to the few. Orgiastic behaviour can be found in all sorts of cultures – from hunter-gatherers (in Australia, for example), to the orgiastic magical rites of hoe-farming cultures (where sometimes all men are demanded to have homosexual sex), to modernity – with its clubs and swingers. We oft accuse Others of orgies: the Wild, Ancestors, Our Children, Americans, Jehova's Witnesses, Hippies, or other groups that don't conform with us.

Sitting in London Euston station one day, I happened upon a book entitled *How to organise an orgy*. I sadly can't remember the author. It was a kind of brochure-guidebook. Maybe it was in a *Do It Yourself* series or came as an extra with some magazine. The authors approached it in a very serious way, for instance discussing whether to send written invitations, in which moment to take clothes off, and how to decide who goes with who. They claim that the main problem at orgies is the low stamina of men, who are completely drained after a few orgasms, leaving a number of women idle. They conclude that the most important thing is to have two men per each woman.

On low sugar

Maybe you're wondering why my notes are so short. Why don't I develop my thoughts into longer treaties? Why not add more details, references, quotes? I can't. I'm writing this book on low sugar. Diabeties runs through my family. Many of my relatives discovered it at 40-50 in already advanced stages. I don't have it yet but I check my sugar with a glucometer every few months, whenever I'm feeling strange. I don't eat sweets or much bread. I eat eggs, salmon, or *al dente* pasta. Actually I am nearly gluten-free as well. I've noticed that in order to write something scientific, something that requires precision of thought, I need my sugar to be above 100 unit, maybe even at 110 or 120. When I come back from a long walk, warmed up, worn out, I am full of quick visions, short thoughts, like the flashes experienced by a warrior on horseback when hunting for game, like the thoughts of someone walking all day, like the dreams of a village shepherd on the verge of starvation. So I put them together. I collect them like leaves from the forest. But I don't feed them with sugar, or chocolate bars, or *cappuccino*, or even a single spoon of sugar in my coffee. I feed them with walking, travel, silence, wormwood tea or normal black tea and lemon, with surprise, yerba, music, night, day, memory.

Hippies and progress

Hippie movements that were strong in the 60s and 70s of the XX century demanded radical changes in lifestyle and awareness. They promoted, among other things, equality, lack of private property, fraternity, love, equal rights, respect for nature. Experimental hippie communes, however, were chiefly unsuccessful, and most ex-hippies created normal families and assimilated into America's economic landscape. But these are only appearances. In reality, many hippie standpoints were adopted by the majority of Western society. Others may reach this point someday. It's probably the same with returning to nature. Many of our current dreams will soon come true while others will not, as it all depends on a ruthless economic calculation. Forty years ago, if I had wanted to be an intellectual or lecturer at a university, I would have had to live in a large city – in Warsaw, Kraków, or Lublin. Today, with the advances of the Internet, phones, and the availability of private vehicles, I can live in a Subcarpathian village, a few hundred metres away from the closest village, surrounded by meadows and forests, and only leave the woods two or three times a week to teach in the city. Of course not everyone lives like this, but many do. Surely this counts as a sort of return.

What else are we missing that would allow for people to be closer to nature and the modal wild human and be possible from an economic point of view?

Definitely more widespread use of natural materials and the slow rejection of plastics and other poisons. A total reform of education: more nature, less sterility. Greater acceptance for nudity – like in Denmark or Germany (paradoxically, one of the least 'natural' nationalities?!). If the number of humans on the planet is stabilised, then a slow move away from farming based on large plantations covered in chemicals. The legalisation of polygamy – accepted by most traditional societies – I don't understand why, as we accept gay marriage, we cannot legalise marriages between one woman and two men or vice versa. The legalization of marijuana. Changes to ways we work, so that most people are self-employed and no-one demands them to work eight hours a day, from a set time to a set time. Most people like to work and will work four or ten hours a day – but why should we do it like slaves, at specific times?

Ash

We now associate ash with dirt, but this didn't used to be the case...

A heap of dirty washing up after we baked a birthday cake for Sarah. A bowl full of greasy mass remains despite the fact I pour hot water and washing up liquid over it. And then I remember camping in the summer and washing dishes with sand and ash. I reach into the ash pan in the fireplace, I throw some ash into the pan and quickly finish washing up.

It was the simplest and the best solution. Have we developed our civilization to exchange ash for washing up liquid?

Modern humans are afraid of ash not only because it would make their clothes dirty. We burn all sorts of crap – plastic and colourful newspapers. We have exchanged clean ash, which is so pleasant to covers ourselves in, for ash that is dirty and without use to anyone.

I'm happy with the progress we've made – with the fact I have electricity and a car – but progress can only be accepted when it doesn't annihilate our primitive resources: clean earth, water, and air, freedom of movement and other human freedoms, the freedom to lie aimlessly in our hammocks for a few hours a day, to spend time with family and friends, close to the forest and water, or to have a fireplace of one's own.

Gypsies

In European culture, Gypsies, i.e. Roma people, are a synonym for wildness. They used to wander without a fixed occupation and without land to cultivate. They have a lot in common with hunter-gatherers, for instance their nomadic lifestyle in small, tight-knit groups. They practiced hunting-gathering, treating farming communities as a foreign ecosystem, and so they hunted for village chickens and collected vegetables grown by other people. Of course not always and not everywhere. They also knew a lot about wild products. In Poland, they collected nettles and ants for soup, and I think in most of Europe they prized hedgehogs baked in clay.

As I mentioned before, Gypsies are not just a nation. They are a symbol, a meme, an idea, a way of life. And so we have unrelated Sea Gypsies in Indochina as well as So-called-Gypsies, New Age Travellers in Great Britain – that is, all sorts of groups of modern 'white' nomads, who travel around the world in car trailers. Someone from the States once told me that they wandered across the continent during the hippie era – to Canada for the summer, to Guatemala for the winter, like a bird.

Wojciech Jóźwiak, an astrologer and dream researcher, claims that the Other often appears in important dreams, sometimes in the form of the Gypsy. I myself had this kind of dream when I was still living in Warsaw and working in the botanical garden. I was in Spain. I ran away from the heat of the sun into a shady narrow street. I saw a small door by the entrance, and next to it, like a column, a two-metre live sturgeon, standing horizontally and winking its eye at me. I went inside. There were three black-haired women there: a young, middle-aged, and old one. The old one walked up to me and said: 'Now you must learn the Gypsy language.' I think it was 1996. It's been fourteen years – and I still haven't learned it. Or maybe it was a metaphor?

Bieszczady

188

The Bieszczady Mountains, nestled in the corner of Poland, adjacent to Slovakia and Ukraine, are currently a symbol of wildness to Poles. Always a little wild and wooded, they became truly wild after the Second World War as a result of fights with the Ukrainian partisans. The Ukrainian inhabitants, the Boykos, were forced to move, leaving abandoned houses and ashes behind. Nearly everything became overgrown with forest. For the past few decades, these have attracted escapees and adventure-seekers, those who wanted to create a new life for themselves – to keep livestock, to play cowboys, mystics, hermits, first inhabitants, or just simply to take drugs in peace.

However, to some, this wild territory can come as a disappointment. Damp, misty valleys covered up to the neck in nettles and alder thickets on abandoned fields. If there were a real primeval forest here, it would be both easier and more pleasant to walk through. There would be large beech trees and less brambles tangling at our feet. Some parts are like this, but these are mostly on the steep northern banks.

We are animals of the savannah. We love large expanses interrupted with individual trees. Many Bieszczady inhabitants complain about the lack of space, remove trees surrounding their houses, allow animals to bite out the terrain and make it savannah-like. I have no large herbivores on my land, except for a few visiting deer, but every year I hire someone with a lawn tractor to mow the area leaving behind single trees – from a distance it looks like a savannah, with birches and alder trees in place of acacias.

The Bieszczady Mountains have now been overrun by four-wheel drives and snobs from Warsaw. Some nature lovers have escaped to the nearby Beskid Niski, i.e. the Low Beskid, but these, advertised by the writer Andrzej Stasiuk, have also become expensive. That's the problem with those who look for the natural – sometimes, they become caricatures of themselves. Just I did, buying a car not long after moving to the countryside. Gurdjieff mentions the way in which self-development is caricatured in Uspienski's *Fragments of an Unknown Teaching*. One of the greatest dangers of development is finding oneself on the opposite pole from the one we started with. Those who search for fortune can end in the gutter, gurus demand money and sex, sportspeople end up with broken limbs, and starving lovers of nature are saved by helicopters and hamburgers.

Shaman

Totalitarianism is one of the greatest dangers to people looking for wildness. States and religions can endeavour to entirely model and control people. An example of direct conflict between Natural Man and totalitarianism is the Inquisition. In many countries, the medieval church led to the craze to remove all traces of past beliefs, rites and magical traditions, and especially traditions which involved the use of psychoactive plants. So-called witches were burned at the stake. Among them, other than entirely accidental innocents, there were many herbalist women who knew ways of using strong psychoactive plants in Europe, for instance henbane, belladonna, and mandrake. The tradition for making hallucinogenic witch balms, along with their recipes, have been lost entirely to the terror of the Middle Ages. Some remains of Middle Age herbalist magic can be seen in Islamic countries. In shops in Marrakesh in Morocco mandrake, harmal (*Peganum harmala*) and other psychoactive plants are still sold by the kilogram. When a shopkeeper saw my then six-month old daughter, he said: 'She's pretty, you need to give her some harmal so no-one curses her with their evil eye.'

Another conflict between Natural Humans and totalitarianism occurred in Stalinist times in Siberia, where local tribal shamans were exterminated.

The word shaman comes from Siberia and was spread into other languages by Russians. It originally meant a Siberian medicine person who cures by entering a trance with the use of a drum and/or the hallucinogenic fly agaric mushroom. The term shaman is usually used in a wider context – to describe any person who attempts to control reality by entering altered states of consciousness, whether spontaneously or through meditation, fasting, physical suffering, lack of sleep, or hallucinogenic substances.

What's the difference between a shaman and a priest? A priest organises rituals, a priest knows, a priest prays. A shaman speaks to spirits and powers directly – mystic priests such as the Franciscan Padre Pio da Pietrelcina (1887-1968) are shamans in this sense.

A large group of anthropologists considers shamanism to be the primitive human religion. The more primitive the tribes we study, the stronger the presence of shamanism. But it must be noted that many groups of hunter-gatherers lack the role of the shaman. However, the shamanic vision of the world is always in the air, and the whole world is

191

filled with ghosts. Animism – a vision of the world as filled with ghosts, spirits, and forces, with which we can go into different relationships (which shamanism is a part of) – is the true primitive religion.

Shamans in Siberia ate fly agarics. However, on the other side of the Pacific, in North America, magicians and great warriors, medicine-men, achieved similar results through fasting, self-harm, and music. It's enough to move further south, to Mexico, to again stumble across shamanic plants of power – peyote, datura, and hallucinogenic mushrooms, described for instance in Carlos Castaneda's fictitious *The Teachings of Don Juan*. Or in more scientific reports, e.g. by the expedition run by Wassons, Hoffman and Heim, which owing the help of the Mazatec healer María Sabina Magdalena García (1894-1985) who uncovered *Psilocybe* mushrooms to them.

Shamans were often taught by older shamans, but could also adopt the role through a spontaneous calling: an ill child who cured itself, a child plagued by spirits wandering through the woods, a person kidnapped by a ghost, completely ruined, eaten up, cut into pieces in their visions – would be put back together as a person of power. In Poland, much was written on shamanism by the deceased professor Andrzej Wierciński (1930-2003), e.g. in his book *Magia i religia* (*Magic and Religion*). I only talked to him and listened to his lectures a few times. After many years out of touch, one night I had a dream. The professor drove up to our house in Rzepnik. It was dawn. I invited him in for a coffee, which we took out to drink under a few-hundred-year-old oak tree that grew next to the church near our house. The professor informed that he came to tell me that he wanted to *kneel in front of this sacred oak and tell me that he likes me.* Then he drove off into the rising sun. I woke up and whispered to Sarah: 'I think Wierciński's dead'. In the morning, my friend called me with the news of the professor's death.

This isn't the only mysterious story I could tell. Sudden flashes of telepathy, synchronous events, contact with souls of the dead and ghosts of trees are normal in human beings who have managed to protect themselves from contamination with our plastic culture.

Shelter

A while back, when striving to be really wild, I built myself a wild year-round shelter. I didn't want a tipi with wind coming through it, so I made a dugout in a steep slope. It was quite big, in fact too big for my building skills (3 x 8 m). I dug 1.5 metres into the earth, covered it with a wooden roof, then with mush and turf. It was a cross between a Slavic dugout, a turf-covered Mandan earth lodge, and a partisan shelter.

It was quite warm but also a little damp and extremely smoky. After a few days inside, I understood that living in it, I'd survive to forty at most. I gave up and after a few months the shelter broke down as the earth started to sink down the trenches in the spring. A double defeat, even though the ruins remained there for the next twelve years. I rose to the surface – living in a small wooden house, I begun to be interested in overground architecture. I built a large shelter covered in dry grass.

Now I live in a different home – a cabin made of logs from a disassembled mid-nineteenth century inn. I cleaned each of these logs with an axe and weatherproofed them myself. I gave the cabin a wild touch. I filled the cracks between logs with moss from the Białowieża Forest. It does better than other fillers. In accord with ancient traditions, on the sides, beneath the logs, I placed coins – one Polish złoty, one British pound, one German and one French Euro. In true EU fashion. I asked for my stove to be made from stones from the river and did not taint either the floor or the walls with any varnish. The wood remained wood. Whenever guests come to visit me, they ask: 'Haven't you thought about impregnating the floor?' 'Well, we're slowly doing it with dirt and grease from our feet'.

Waves

As anyone who has had an EEG knows, brain waves are measurable cycles of bioelectrical brain activity. Gamma waves (40-100 Hz) occur when we are physically active. Slower ones – beta (around 12-28 Hz) – correspond to daily life. Alpha – 8-13 Hz – are waves of rest, relaxation, which occur when we're lying down with our eyes closed and are used for fast learning. Then there are theta – 4-5 Hz – shamanic waves – the border of waking life and dream states, where the ability to think rationally ends and visions begin. These are the waves of suggestiveness, waves in which we can control our own physiological functions. Finally, there is delta – 0,5 to 3 Hz – waves of sleep and deep meditation.

In modern life, we spend too much time in gamma and beta, and too little in alpha, theta, and delta. We lack

194

sleep, dreams, shamanic visions, and peace. It's not just through pharmacology that our brain can be made to enter different wave states. The drum is a great tool – around two hundred beats per minute transport us into a world of shamanic visions, and slower drumming is calming and puts us to sleep.

This doesn't mean that our wild ancestors slept and dreamt well. Uncomfortable shelters, crying children, rodents, snakes, and mosquitos disturbed them. The title of Everett's book, *Don't sleep, there are snakes*, perfectly exemplifies the specifics of the realities of tribal life in the Amazon. As Everett writes, life goes on around the clock. There's someone waking up and making noise all the time. In this state, there are probably more *theta* than *delta* waves. Someone once said that in order to survive in the temperate climate, you have to constantly think about the future, and to survive in the tropical rainforest climate, you have to constantly think about the present and its dangers.

I live in a temperate climate – in a Carpathian village lost between hills. I have to think about firewood, winter tyres, and investments for the future. There's snow outside my window. I sit in a comfortable chair with my feet on the table. My arm is in plaster (not enough attention paid in daily life, I slipped on ice). I perform an examination of my conscience in relation to my return to nature, I eat saffron milk caps I marinated myself and listen to a DVD of drumming at some Plains Indians' dance. I float away, I drift off, then suddenly I hear a humming. The sink is blocked and the washing has streamed out of the washing machine hose and flooded the kitchen. *Don't sleep, there are snakes.*

Straight and crooked

In nature, most things are crooked. Few trees are straight. Some branches and blades of grass are, but rarely perfectly. There's always that barely noticeable crookedness, like in a block of wood hewed with an axe. Even while driving a car you can see from two hundred metres away whether a log has been hand-hewn or whether it's come from a sawmill. The Chinese, in accord with the laws of *feng shui*, believe that long, ideally straight lines are damaging in a landscape. They create the deadly *sha* energy which leads to misfortune and illness. However, a straight line bound in a square or wide rectangle is beautiful. A rectangular field is the ideal counterbalance to the chaos of the jungle. One rectangle, one circle of shelters on the prairie – these are beautiful, but we have changed the world into a whole labyrinth of straight lines. The beauty of old architecture lies not just in patina and spirit. Sometimes it's simply a matter of crookedness. It can be enough to buy the builder a drink, tell them to be less exact– and they'll begin to build like in the olden days. An oval art nouveau-style sign, a horseshoe, rounded corners, are enough to make us feel better. In the modern world, only the English have maintained a sensitivity to the crooked.

Those horrible sharp corners. Driving through Poland I see houses plastered with edges like razors. Couldn't we make things softer? Just a little blunt. A building is natural when it's built roughly, by hand, with an axe, out of clay, wood, recycled brick. To create patina on a brick wall the English pour milk over it to make moss grow on it.

196

But why go as far as Britain to talk about *feng shui*? The crooked has a strong presence in our Polish folk traditions, but we're ashamed of it and have negated it. The traces of Polish folk wisdom remain in the landscape – animal-shaped carvings on roofs, stones on doorsteps, and fanciful ornaments around windows. Leszek Matela writes well on this subject in his book *Polskie feng-shui* (*Polish Feng-shui*).

Children of the Mayans

One of the things that separates modern humans from hunter-gatherers or even primitive farmers is the latter's deep knowledge of their environment. Although wild humans don't go to school, they know most species of plants and animals that surround them. They have names for them which are their own, local, but not so different from scientific names. Very often a tribe's taxonomy of the living world corresponds nearly perfectly to the scientific. Sometimes the tribal classification is more precise, when it concerns organisms most crucial for survival, for instance cultivated plants or fish. In such cases, the wild distinguish between different kinds of one scientific species. In other cases, this folk classification can be less precise. For example moss, for individual species of which names are usually lacking, although their diversity is signalled in an unspoken way.

This knowledge of the environment is acquired from early childhood through making plants into toys – wreaths out of flowers, string out of stalks, bags out of bark, animals out of leaves. It is passed on when picking berries with mothers and sisters, hunting with fathers, catching fish in your hands with friends.

This direct knowledge of the environment is available not only to the wild, but also, until recently, to people who grew up cow herding – simple peasants in run-down corners of Poland were nearly as rich in this knowledge as primitive tribes.

Such forms of knowledge are dying out. Children who are brought up in front of computer screens, flocked into classrooms, and protected from getting dirty by thick biology teachers, don't really know about nature. They are taught genetics, life cycles, lists of protected species, but they are not shown what lies behind the garden fence. Peacock butterfly caterpillars feeding on nettle, common knotgrass they pass on the path, trees in the park, or the species of tits which eat the fruit off bushes unknown to them in front of their flats.

In traditional societies, children's knowledge of nature is immense. Stross led research on children from the Tzeltzal Maya people.[22] There were around two hundred genera of plants on a path. At the age of four, children were able to name thirty-two species of plants, at the age of nine as many as 106 genera and twenty species. Repeated research a few years ago from Zarger and Stepp showed no substantial decrease in this knowledge in the last thirty years.[23] Hunn has run similar research. A twelve year old

---

[22] Stross, B. 1973. Acquisition of botanical terminology by Tzeltal children. In: *Meaning in Mayan Languages*. M.S. Edmonson (ed.). The Hague: Mouton, pp. 107-141.

[23] Zarger, R.K., Stepp, J.R. 2004. Persistence of botanical knowledge among Tzeltal Maya children. *Current Anthropology,* 45(3): 413-418.

girl from the Zapotec people in the state of Oaxaca in Mexico was able to describe the uses of 383 taxa of plants, which is apparently typical of this tribe.[24] Children in the USA know only a fraction of the number of species that children from indigenous Mexican tribes do.

The problem currently lies in the fact that not only do children not know the names of plants, but that they are scared to give names to them themselves. Carol Kaesuk Yoon has brought this to attention in her book *Naming Nature*. People are naturally inclined to name and classify living things. The task at hand isn't to force children to learn names of plants, but to teach them the joys of naming, the joys of spontaneous manipulation of the world, while in European school, they are taught powerlessness and passivity.

What strikes me is that it seems that hunter-gatherers supposedly know less species of plants which grow around them than agricultural societies[25]. Thus we cannot think that hunter-gatherers knew EVERYTHING. No, they were one with the environment, but they definitely knew animals better than plants.

---

[24] Hunn. E.S. 2002. Evidence for the precocious acquisition of plant knowledge by Zapotec children. In: *Ethnobiology and Biocultural Diversity*. J.R. Stepp, F.S. Wyndham, R.K. Zarger (ed.). International Society of Ethnobiology, Athens, GA, pp. 604-613.

[25] Brown, C.H., Anderson Jr, E.N., Bulmer, R., Drechsel, P., Ellen, R.F., Hays, T.E., Headland, T.N., Howe, L., Hyndman, D.C., Jensen, K.E. and Morris, B., 1985. Mode of subsistence and folk biological taxonomy [and comments and reply]. *Current Anthropology*, 26(1), pp.43-64.

Breasts

I forgot about another attribute of wildness: human milk. One of the most important symptoms of the development of civilization was depriving us of the option of feeding on our mother's milk in the first months and years of our lives. The replacement of natural human milk (with a protein, fat, and sugar content optimal for the child's development) with man-made foods reached its peak a few decades after World War II. Now we are returning to this food.

Amongst contemporary hunter-gatherers who breastfeed (or rather used to breastfeed, because there are barely any of them left) their children for a few years of their life, it is normal to feed for five-six years. Of course, full nutritional dependency of the child on the mother lasts only for the first year (often less), but it is nevertheless the cases that the wild woman often made use of her breast.

A few different aspects of humans' escape from nature have their meeting point in the female breast. First of all, distrust of natural food. In the second half of the XX century, breast milk was considered insufficient – too watery, occurring in too small quantities, and the act of breastfeeding itself – unhygienic and unnatural. Secondly, hiding breasts, which are the fountain of the first human food and a symbol of womanhood. The negation of the natural, but also of the erotic aspect of breasts. On the other hand, women's fear of revealing them in order not to excite dangerous, aggressive, patriarchal males.

We must keep all of our organs active to stay healthy. It is using them, and the flow of energy through each of

200

them, that makes us agile and protects us from cancer. Of course I mean use, not overuse or exploitation. Women who breastfeed for a few years are less likely to develop breast cancer. Men who ejaculate often are less likely to get prostate cancer. As for joints, people who practice yoga can preserve elasticity of their joints up to old age, which protects them from injuries and enables them to lead fully active lives. In middle age, we usually start to completely give ourselves over to automatic, chiefly sedentary activities. Repeating the same positions over and over completely stiffens us and puts a strain on our bones and muscles. Children are different: they jump, wriggle around, lie on the floor, shake their legs around, climb trees and make dozens of all sorts of other different moves. Jesus' words: 'be like children' have another dimension: 'be loose, diverse, natural, use all of your organs, just sensibly!'

Wild woman

I have already written about wild women building their wigwams and not being afraid of nudity, about wild Agta women who hunt for wild pigs, about wild Aché women who change husbands dozens of times, but there is another category I haven't touched upon: wild women who own horses. I have met a few in my life. A large number of women who have a primitive energy, strength, courage, and love for nature, are fascinated with horse riding.

Are horses a symbol of wildness? Not to me. Primitive hunter-gatherers didn't own them. The move towards horses did give the first riders a great advantage over those on foot, both in terms of speed of movement and the ability to transport goods. Hence, Plains Indians took over horses from Europeans. They could then colonise empty and unhospitable parts of the plains. Before, they existed on its fringes, by the rivers, at the edges of forests.

Nevertheless, a horse is wild in comparison to a car or a bicycle.

Maybe teenage girls' fascination with horses is an element of their budding sexuality? One of these wild women with a horse told me that she had her first orgasm while galloping on her horse. For a woman, a horse signifies the search for strength, for power, and maybe the desire to be men's equals. And then the smell of the horse apparently turns them on.

'Do you have any stallion-scented perfumes?'

'I'm sorry, sir, we don't.' The woman makes an expression that combines surprise, disgust, an attempt to stop an attack of laughter, and sexual interest.

The horse is also important in dreams. In many dream books, it is a symbol of death, mystery, and transformation. Surprisingly, they also appear in my own dreams – the dreams of a man who finds horses, cats, and dogs annoying. I will tell you one of them.

I dreamt of one of my beloved spots – a white chapel on the top of Wólka Bratkowska on the Dynów Hills. I always pass it on my way from home to Krosno. Other people are also drawn to it. My younger daughter, by the age of three, would shout, whenever we would go up it: 'This is my favourite hill!'. And indeed, it's a very special place. In very fine weather (like on a few neighbouring hills in Rzepnik, Bratkówka, Odrzykoń, Korczyna, and Kombornia) you can see a whole panorama of the Carpathians, from the Bieszczady alpine meadows, through

202

the Lower Beskids, the majestic Slovakian Tatras, all the way to the corners of the Western Beskids.

The chapel is white and next to it there's a birch tree and a linden tree. The hill is treeless and with a beautiful panorama. In the dream, however, part of the hill, all the way up to the top, was covered in beech forests. Five thin white horses and five gigantic overfed rats were tied to the chapel. I cut them off. The animals smiled at me and slowly made their way off into the forest.

On the edge of the forest, they were met by a massive stallion. And now every time I sit down by that chapel, I think about that dream. I name my Dynów Hills the Wild Boar Hills.

What disgusting, 'unnatural' names: the Dynów Hills, the Strzyżów-Dynów Hills, or the Czarnorzeki-Strzyżów Landscape Park. I would like to put Wild Boar Hills on the map. A mysterious, entangled chain of hills and valleys, from Kombornia to Mount Chełm, like a sleeping dragon towering over Krosno. One of its eyes is the Kamieniec Castle, the other – the Prządki rocks.

Hills

Witek and Ania escaped the city fifteen years ago. They were looking for their place, living in a Volkswagen Transporter and renting out different huts. In the end, they bought an old house off the beaten track. Within a few years' time, they converted it into a true wooden palace. They expanded it with canopies, conservatories, added a greenhouse and converted the stable into guest rooms. The mountains were their sacred space. When they were tired of collecting blackthorn for sale, they lay down on the grass in front of their hut, knowing that they were where they were meant to be. They spent hours in the wind, hearing the thud of fruit falling into their plastic buckets. They could see buzzards, hawks, and even eagles fly past. In the summer, they gathered herbs for a herbal tea company: St John's wort, agrimony, linden and eyebright. In the evenings, they were covered in sweat. But their skin smelled not only salty, but absorbed the fragrance of thyme, St John's wort and mint. It smelled of summer. It was covered in small red dots, signs of slight allergies to grass, insect bites, mosquito bites, and red rings made by brambles.

Once they had children, they needed more money. He taught English in a private school in town, she taught Russian here in the village. Their magical world of the seasons shrank a bit – there was no time for gathering bouquets of cowslips and lungworts in spring. There was no time for mushroom picking in the autumn. They took any extra hours they could to be able to finish the cottage. They didn't go skiing. They didn't chop their own wood up or even paint their home themselves anymore. There was always someone without a job in the village willing to do it for a bottle of spirits.

They only had the summer to themselves. They treated the summer holidays as sacred. That's when they had time to themselves and for the forest. They picked ceps and chanterelles in August. They swam in the river.

In the end, they finished renovating their hut and the children grew up a little. They bought sheep and started offering rooms for tourists. They had a lot of guests who were delighted with the views, the sheep cheese and delicious preserves. They adored the heavenly atmosphere –

insofar as it is possible to make in this climate, where rain falls for a few months every year and the sky is grey as steel two hundred days a year.

As soon as I met them, I thought: what a great place for a conference. I needed one at the time. The participants were delighted. Their stomachs bulged from trying ever-new specialties from the kitchen cupboard. After lectures, they lay on the grass, basking in the sun, or wandered around the forest nearby, bringing back armfuls of unexpected mushroom findings wrapped up in their T-shirts.

We're sitting on the terrace, drinking wonderful coffee, some Mexican brand Witek found on the Internet. A dot appears on the horizon.

'Who's that?' I ask.

'The woman who picks ceps for my guests' Witek replies. 'I haven't been to the forest myself for two years,' he adds. 'No, I mean, I got that wrong, I went in January in the four-wheel drive to get some wood,' he then boasts. 'It's hard to get out because we keep having guests, but I've bought myself a trip to the safari in Africa, I'm going with both of my sons.'

I phone Witek a few months later:

'How was the safari?'

'Great,' he answers. 'I saw so many animals I'd dreamt of seeing. I walked the earth that was home to the first humans. I recharged energetically. But too bad that while I was telling the English about our Polish wolves, they ate all my sheep. If I hadn't gone to the safari, I would have finally seen them in real life.'

Witek has an interesting neighbour in the village. Edward also collected plants and mushrooms, but he fell in

205

love with the hallucinogenic ones. He did well for the first few years. He sold them in student halls in Kraków. The mountains were especially rich in *Psilocybe semilanceata* and another species I won't name, so that those f***ers don't put them down on some list of forbidden species. The former are small, whitish, with sharp tops. The latter are dark and bell-shaped. They loved to grow on Witek's fields, among the sheep dung. He made more money on them – in fact, ten times more – than Witek did on his milk sheep cheese. He also lived in a hut on a hill, he bought an old four-wheel drive, some Russian UAZ on the verge of falling apart. He was often visited by girls but was never with any of them for long. He was handsome, beautiful, with long thick dark dreadlocks. He not only sold magic mushrooms – he loved them. He ate them on his bread and butter. He liked regularity. Yunnan tea, black pudding and bread with butter and mushrooms. Sometimes, when he was out of them, he would spread honey and fried *Psilocybe* on the bread. He ate his breakfast on the front step of his hut – a tall step of the kinds that used to be made to stop evil from entering the house.

After eating that bread, he could see Jesus over his hill. And the blue of infinity. His land below it. Sometimes completely altered. More colourful than the way most people see it. Faces appeared in the bark of trees. It was especially beautiful in the spring, when birdsong was transformed into rainbow figures and smudges of colour. Sometimes he was under the impression that he had not two eyes but one. That this One eye – perhaps his Third eye – spanned the whole world, from Africa to Antarctica, the Pacific and the Arctic, that it turned back and massaged his back. Maybe he turned into a Three-eyed Raven from the

Game of Thrones? He could feel the skeletons of previous generations under his doorstep – cold ghosts of the soil and hot, dangerous forces of hell which he believed in. This went on for three years.

One day, thunder struck his hut. But Edward liked stability. He didn't want to move out. He moved to the barn which remained intact. He put in a stove and insulated it with wool. His health deteriorated, he even started receiving benefits. But he still smiled a lot and radiated goodness. He would give anything to other people. He was warm, as if beaming with some aura. 'The mushrooms softened me,' he said.

He kept eating bread with mushrooms. He sat on his doorstep and looked at the rising sun. He always said his prayers, with a particular emphasis on the line 'give us this day our daily bread'.

When I last saw him, his dreadlocks were going grey. Other than that, he was unchanged. After two beers he sat down under the table and began to play the drum and mutter for hours on end. He was in the zone.

Runner's Rush

Runner's Rush, Runner's High, or Runner's Euphoria is a euphoric state which occurs during a long run or another long-term physical activity and causes increased resistance to pain and tiredness. The theory was formed in the seventies. First it was attributed to so-called endorphins. These substances, produced by our bodies, are inner analogues to morphine. They are produced in larger quantities during prolonged efforts and after injuries, but also when falling in love (only for a few weeks…) or eating meals rich in chilli.

According to current opinion on the importance of physical activity to human health, it is best to exercise for over an hour a day. Only exercise that lasts longer than three quarters of an hour makes us use up the glycogen stored in our muscles and move to anaerobic respiration. Oxygen deficiency causes stress to the body, which may in turn lead to a large release of endorphins. Regular using up of the stores of glycogen is also the best method for natural weight loss.

The endorphin theory is sometimes put under question, as the mood enhancement experienced after running is experienced even by people who have been given endorphin inhibitors. It is assumed that a few different substances come to form the runner's high phenomenon, including cannabinoids and phenethylamine which is related to amphetamine.

Although primitive people sometimes had a few lazy days in a row when there was food and the weather was bad, they were still a lot more active than we currently are. It is probably the lack of movement that has caused the wave of depression flooding the rich West. There's a paradox here. Currently, people who live in the countryside and drive to work in the city move less than people from the centre of town, who walk everywhere. There is often no reason to move in the countryside. There's only one road and running along it is boring. And the city? The city is a network of roads in which energy moves through many channels. Someone once said a city is like a crystal. It's a place where energy flows in a regular way that is beneficial to humans.

The Earth is ours

There was once a massive, beautiful pond. Julek dug it with a spade. In fourteen years, he built a four-metre dam. This pond was the pearl of the village. Although it was yellow, the water was clean, fragrant, and came from a spring. Dragonflies flew around the bulrushes, and a fifty-metre swim across it was a real adventure. But one day the bailiff took Julek's pond away – it was too long. They auctioned it and the pond was bought by a certain gentleman from Silesia.

One day I arrived at the pond with a towel, as I did almost every day in the summer. The pond wasn't there. Diggers and bulldozers were wading through the mud. The pond was being deepened. Now it's bigger, deeper, and exactly square, to keep order. Another time I went there, it had already been fenced. The metal poles, enforced with concrete, glimmered in the sun like soldiers. There was a net between them with a sign on it: 'Private property, no entry'.

I guess the Silesian wasn't even that bothered by people using his pond. He did it out of fear, because the Polish law stupidly makes the owner of the pond responsible for whoever drowns in it unless it's fenced. Yet another example of the idiocy of the laws in the country I live in.

It's true, plenty of people nearly drowned in that pond. Mietek, Franek, Władek, me. They got cramp or they were drunk. There was also a shack by the pond. The youths would go there for obvious reasons.

Primitive people didn't have the concept of private property. Land could at most belong to the tribe, but in a different sense than it does now. The borders between the land of tribes X and Y were rarely sharp. Sometimes they only concerned holy places, graves, or specific habitats of animals and plants. There were no polygons on the map – countries, counties, fields – but points – campsites, holy places, and paths. The rest was free.

Presently, the approach to use of private land in different countries of the Civilised World is varied. In Poland, it is completely normal to go mushroom picking and collect herbs in forests and wastelands without considering who the land might belong to. Part of the forests are state-owned, part private, but no-one's too concerned about this. But setting up a tent is a different matter. I've heard so many stories about foresters harassing some traveller innocent as a lamb. Still, before the Second World War you had to buy a ticket to pick anything from the undergrowth in the forest.

In England, it's the opposite. Before we enter some territory, we first need to think about who it belongs to. If we enter a private pasture, they probably won't shoot us immediately, but who knows what could happen. Britain is a feudal country. Most of the land belongs to a small group of aristocracy and farmers. For many years now, there has been a campaign to open up access to these large estates, which are often walled up and usually hidden behind hedges. The English landscape, divided with ancient hedges, is in its nature less accessible to outsiders. We are allowed to move along specially designated paths which even have special stairs leading over the hedges and gates so that we don't end up letting the sheep out. In Scotland there is already greater freedom for hillwalking guaranteed by the law. Scandinavia is a true paradise for wandering freely. Not only is there a lot of free space, but they have a special old law operative in Norway (Allemannsretten), Sweden (Allemansrätten), and Finland (Jokamiehenoikeus), which guarantees freedom of movement, and even the right for a traveller to pitch their tent and start a fire for the night.

Burn the books

People from Bratkówka told me about how they looted the Starowiejski's manor. The lords were chased away when communist times came after World War II. The furniture was moved downstream all the way to the villages of Łączki and Łęki. In many manors such as this one, books and furniture were used as firewood. There is something barbaric, horrid, repulsive, but also tempting about this.

When I wanted to escape to the forest my books were the biggest obstacle. Sensitive to damp and the smallest drop of rain, they have to be protected, which uses up energy. When I started thinking about moving to the woods, the first thing I did was organise my bookshelves. Even if I couldn't get rid of it all, I reduced it to works worth saving for posterity. I burned my old school books, old guidebooks and notebooks in a fire. Out of six hundred books, I selected three hundred for sale in one night. 'This is real, genuine literary criticism' – Zbyszek, the owner of an antique book store, laughed mockingly. For example, I sold all of my Czesław Miłosz books – I got bored of him. What remained were, among others, plant identification guides, cookbooks, encyclopaedias, and XIX-century family prayer books. As for novels, I kept only Adams' *Watership Down*, J.R.R. Tolkien, and Boris Vian.

They took up only a few boxes and could now be taken to the end of the world.

After finishing my PhD I experienced such repulsion towards the written word that I didn't write a single thing for two years, other than filling out forms at the post office and doing my tax returns. I taught English and collected seeds. It was a wonderful break which ended with me writing my first book, *Wild edible plants of Poland*, published in 2002.

However, if I were to stay in the forest for years, I would really miss these books, especially good scientific articles. Good science reaches the heights of the best art. Maybe one day all the laptops will be waterproof and shockproof, so lasting that we might be able to log into a library on the other side of the world and crush nuts in the forest with the same device? And of course they will be charged by solar power. I wrote these words in 2009. Now in 2019 a large part of the population has large water-proof smartphones – ideal for woodland hermits, particularly if they have photovoltaic solar panels and wi-fi -. Recently a journalist from Warsaw interviewed me for a book about people seeking wilderness. She complained that all the to-be-hermits had smartphones and Internet. I don't think that she was right. There ARE some people getting rid of them. But she was herself trapped in searching for the 'wild people' using her social media contacts. To find one, she would to step out of the matrix. I actually knew one or two who surely did not have a cell phone but did not bother to tell her. Let them be real hermits forgotten by the world.

Simplification and complication

In the different aspects of looking for wildness and naturalness described here, there is a clash of two tendencies: towards simplification and increasing diversity.

Some want to 'return to nature' because their life seems too complicated. They think that people were happier when they led 'simpler' lives (implying simple households, clothing, and repetition of a few tasks throughout one's life). Others see the progress of civilization in terms of impoverishment: the disappearance of biodiversity, languages, and ecosystems. So a return to nature would mean the protection of biodiversity, an escape from corporate imprisonment or years of work as a salesperson, labourer, or graphic designer, and an attempt to complicate one's life: exchange work in front of the computer with chopping wood, collecting fruits, beekeeping, maybe cultivating vegetables, the practice of some crafts, etc.

In the evolution of human society, there is a tendency to replace simple arrangements with more complex ones. XIX century evolutionists noticed this and although the next generations of anthropologists ridiculed them for it, this way of thinking is currently being returned to, and attention brought to the fact that this gradual complication of societies creates more food. It is the increased production of food that is the main determinant factor in the evolution of societies.

And so sadly our attempts to flee into nature are limited by this extremely important factor: amount of food. We cannot get past this limitation.

The complicated systems we create – cities, technologies, farming systems – ruin other complicated systems such as forests or coral reefs. Our task ought to be the creation of a harmonious state in which all of civilizations' achievements can be preserved together with all habitats. One of the solutions, other than the classic techniques of wildlife conservation, should be the castration of people who have had four children. Sorry, there's already more than enough people on Earth!

To snow

In search for nature, I ran away to the countryside. I spend the winter in front of my computer – connected to humanity by a few hundred metre underground Internet and phone cable. I am, however, surrounded by beautiful wilderness: wild forests, streams, and meadows. I spend a lot of money each month on petrol to get to town and the shop. Was it worth it? Would it not be better to live in a small room in a Warsaw flat? To go for walks by the Vistula and collect wild vegetables in meadows on the outskirts of Warsaw? To participate to the human community in a natural way: in a coffee shop or a room in my institute? Was it worth exchanging these for untainted nature, silence, the necessity of owning a car or talking to people via the computer screen? In my case it was, but in writing these words, I wanted to show that living in the country is not the only natural way. An inhabitant of the city can nowadays be just as close to nature. That which is the most wild and primitive, and what is the most modern, sometimes goes hand in hand in the strangest ways. Take

Moroccan herbalists, who use powdered CDs (and now maybe DVDs) to improve memory, alongside dried chameleons for regaining sanity. So I close my computer, open the door and, for balance, break into a run onto the large expanse of the snowy hill.

Sarah is wild

Sarah hates it when I call her Sara. The slight difference in English pronunciation, and the one troublesome letter at the end, are often a source of marital disagreements. Despite her attachment to letters, Sarah is wild. She appeared in my life like the jinn out of Alladin's lamp. Like a conjured spirit. I write these words exactly in the place where this jinn first surfaced – the district of Kazimierz in Kraków. Until now, I didn't consider including her in this book. I just didn't think of it until I came here, to the beginning.

Nearly 24 years ago, in 1996, I came here, to bar Singer on Estery Street, for the first time. I was with my sister and her friend Marcin. We made a toast of kosher plum vodka. A ray of February light came in through the window to this gloomy place. Some photos fell out of Marcin's wallet like tarot cards. One was a picture of Sarah standing in some yogic as black-haired and black-browed face I sa intelligence, warmth, terror, and weakness sked for her address. Marcin have it to me me mockingly: 'She's an English poet, she sterday, you'll probably never meet'.

215

We exchanged letters. I once decided to phone her from a phone booth (this was the pre-mobile, very-early-stage Internet era). Eight zlotys for three minutes on the phone. *This is so financially reckless* – I thought – *it would be great if the booth didn't take coins.* And it didn't. We talked for free for two hours. I kept being interrupted by people standing in line to the phone. And then we ended up living together.

Sarah is wild because she laughs. Most travellers to different poor, wild, hot countries make this observation: people laugh there. She laughs like she's from the centre of the jungle. She doesn't have survival skills, other than knowing how to properly pitch a tent. She doesn't know wild plants, she doesn't kill animals, and she can only light a fire using matches. But if some awful catastrophe occurred, only she and the rats would survive. She is centred. *I scoop the loop*, she says. She's present, she's in herself. She exists, she lives, and she is within, not outside herself. While I would search for food, she would starve and probably survive me.

We actually split up four years ago, but this does not change what I wrote here. Now she lives in Glasgow, Scotland. She is in a city, but she is still a wild being. She doesn't drive. She walks everywhere, and in this city of parks it is possible to live like a squirrel. I visit her frequently and forage there as well. I pick beechnuts and ground elder in Queen's Park, collect service berries on Victoria Road, and find sweet cicely and hogweed along city streams.

Sarah is wild because she hates having pictures taken. I only don't like it a little bit, but she hates it with a passion.

Sarah is wild because she gives herself to the situation with her whole self.

Sarah is wild because she breastfed our daughter Nasim for five years and three months, and our second daughter, Daisy, for three month longer. A true dairy farm.

Sarah is wild because she loves rhythm.

Sarah is wild because she loves red. She always looks either like a fuchsia, or a rose, or a peony.

Sarah is wild because she is.

Sarah is wild and it was she who taught me that searching for wildness is a load of nonsense one should engage in with one's whole heart.

Epilogue

Not so long ago, not as long ago as in Dukla, in fact quite recently, I was wandering along the Jasiołka river in a village near the town of Jasło. Just like I describe at the beginning of this book, I was surrounded by fields of wild garlic. Just as in Dukla, I picked on its leaves, and as in Dukla, an elderly person walked up to me. This time it was me who asked:

'Good day, what are you doing?'

'Pickin' garlic,' the elderly stranger answered.

'Bear's garlic?' I asked.

'What do you mean, bear's garlic,' the old man replied. 'it's wild, wild garlic. The priest started pickling it in jars, so the women also started doing it, so my woman also sent me. It's good for everything, 'cause it's wild, strong.'

.

Made in the USA
Middletown, DE
28 December 2020